How to Study Poker

Volume 1: Techniques For Making You A Better Player Today Than You Were Yesterday

Sky Matsuhashi

How To Study Poker

How to Study Poker
Volume 1: Techniques For Making You A Better Player Today Than You Were Yesterday

Copyright © 2017 Sky Matsuhashi
Published by Smart Poker Study Publications
www.SmartPokerStudy.com
Printed in the United States of America

All rights reserved. No part of this publication may be reproduced, distributed, or transmitted in any form or by any means, including photocopying, recording, or other electronic or mechanical methods, without the prior written permission of the publisher, except in the case of brief quotations embodied in reviews and certain other non-commercial uses permitted by copyright law.

ISBN 978-1-946965-00-4 paperback
ISBN 978-1-946965-01-1 audiobook
ISBN 978-1-946965-02-8 eBook

Cover Design by:
Colin Brennan
www.behance.net/colinbrennan

TABLE OF CONTENTS

Acknowledgements	vi
1. How This Book Will Help You	1

Part I: The Poker Student Mindset — 9

2. Characteristics Of Great Poker Minds	10
3. Developing Skills To The Level Of Unconscious Competence	17
4. Improving Poker Skills With Purposeful Practice	21
5. Utilizing The Learning Process Model	25
6. Directing Your Studies By Asking Great Questions	29

Part II: Plan Your Poker Journey In Six Steps — 36

7. Step 1. Determine Where You Want Poker To Take You	37
8. Step 2. Set SMART Poker Goals	38
9. Step 3. Choose The Necessary Skills That Will Get You There	44
10. Step 4. Create A Weekly Plan For Improving Your Game	49
11. Step 5. Keep A Journal & Track Your Progress	59
12. Step 6. Build Strong Poker Play And Study Habits	65

How To Study Poker

Part III: Study Techniques For In-Game Work 68

13. Poker Session Warm-ups & Cooldowns 69

14. Control Tilt With Logic Statements 73

15. FOCUS Sessions: Building Skills While Playing 78

16. Volume Sessions: Learning While Earning 82

17. Game Tape: The Most Underutilized Yet Beneficial Study Technique 87

Part IV: Study Techniques For Off-The-Felt Work 93

18. Utilizing 25 Different (And Simple) Study Techniques 94

19. Getting The Most From PokerTracker 4: The Best Suite Of Online Tools 103

20. PokerTracker 4: Common Statistics For Analysis 117

21. Getting The Most From Flopzilla: The Best Calculating Software 125

22. Hand History Reviews For Analyzing Your Game And Finding Leaks 133

23. Learning From Poker Strategy Content 137

24. Teaching Poker To Learn 146

Free Workbook Offer!

DOWNLOAD THE WORKBOOK FOR "HOW TO STUDY POKER" FOR FREE!

Just to say thank you for buying this book, I'd like to give you the 30-page Workbook PDF for "How To Study Poker" 100% FREE

DOWNLOAD FREE HERE

http://www.smartpokerstudy.com/HTSPfreeoffer

Acknowledgements

I could not have written this book without a ton of help.

A special thanks to my family: Denise, Mason and Dalen. Your encouragement and love mean the world to me. Thanks as well to my brother Dusty for all the encouragement and technical expertise in publishing this book.

I want to thank Alan Schmidt for the bang-up job he did proofreading and editing my book. This book is so much improved thanks to his input, which I value greatly. Any mistakes remaining are solely mine.

Tom Fazio, Matt Tagliaferri and Dennis Pedersen deserve praise as well for their great insights into ideas that made this book stronger.

Thank you to all who support me on Patreon: Dennis Pedersen and Adam Wandler – thanks for being there for all of my webinars. Alan Schmidt and Price Keene – you guys rock. Wayne Hendersen, Robson Ribeiro, Mike Tappert, John Blank, Mrs. Anonymous, John Prehn, Pere Masramon, Eric Strachan and Dustin Heiner – I'm so appreciative of your support and I'll keep delivering for all of you

— 1 —
How This Book Will Help You

"If you want to change the world, pick up your pen and write."
-Martin Luther

I don't want to change *the world*, just *your poker world*.

This book is intended for all online and LIVE players like me who want to use the online realm to improve their poker games. Online poker allows for playing hundreds of thousands of hands per year, software to record and study all those hands, training sites that make learning very simple and quick community connections to share information and to help everyone grow together.

When I started playing poker in 2003, I did what most beginners do to learn the game: I just played a ton of LIVE poker. I was learning through experience. I spent all of my free time at a couple of local cardrooms and home games. Eventually, I made my way from the brick and mortar cardrooms to the online rooms of PokerStars and Ultimate Bet.

It took me a while (four years or so), but I eventually concluded that to crush these games, I needed more than just playing. So I picked up some poker books. *Super System*, *Elements of Poker* and *Winning Low-Limit Hold'em* were just a few of the titles. These books taught me many concepts and strategies that I didn't learn at the tables. They laid out a solid foundation (and in some cases a pretty dated foundation), but one that was just built upon the word of the pros who wrote them. I needed more, I needed to learn how to learn the game of poker. I needed to be able to find the answers for myself. But where to go?

"There's poker training online?"

In the '08 Main Event broadcasts, at one point Norman Chad was talking about some kid with the screen name "LuckyChewy". And when I say kid, I mean it; he looked like a 14-year-old illegally playing in a casino. Norman (we're on a first name basis, I call him Norman and he calls me Guy) said this kid was a coach at an online poker training website.

HOLD THE PHONE!

"There's poker training online? How come nobody ever told me? And how the heck is this kid a coach!" I didn't know it at the time, but "LuckyChewy" is Andrew Lichtenberger who won the 2010 World Series of Poker Circuit and was born in 1987, so he was a baby-faced 21 year old during the broadcast.

Of course, there's online training for anything that people want to get better at, poker included. It just never occurred to me. Remember, this was back in 2008 and the internet wasn't what it is today; the first place you go to learn anything. What has two thumbs and can be an ignoramus? This guy.

Talk about pivotal, eye opening, mind-blowing … a watershed moment for me!

I immediately went to the computer and discovered a whole new world … PocketFives … Cardrunners … Two Plus Two … Pokertrixx.com (remember that one?).

I started watching my first training videos, reading poker strategy articles and participating in forums. My game continued to improve, I started to learn and earn more, and even enjoy the game more. Then I realized something.

All of the poker content I consumed taught me strategy, but it never taught me how to develop my own strategies. That was a huge problem as I saw it!

I had to infer from what they were discussing how I could work this stuff out away from the tables for myself. Plus, if everyone reading these books employed the same strategies I was, then isn't the only winner going to be the house?

I needed to figure out how to devise my own strategies and understand the underlying principles on my own.

As the old saying goes, "Give a man a fish and you feed him for a day, teach him to fish and you feed him for a lifetime." These videos and articles were giving me fish all day every day, but they weren't showing me where in the ocean to find them,

How This Book Will Help You

nor how to string my own line, nor how to drive the boat. They weren't even directing me to the bait shop!

I needed more! So I embarked on a journey of poker self-improvement. Along the way I developed study strategies and on-the-felt practices geared toward teaching myself to fish. I continued to watch training videos and read articles and books, but I would read between the lines and figure out ways that I could discover the professionals' secrets for myself.

Yes, You Need To Learn How To Study

Some of you might be thinking: *Geez, I don't need to learn how to study. I watch videos, read forums and play a ton. What more is there to studying poker?*

There's quite a bit more, but only as much as you're willing to put yourself through.

This book will show you how to improve your game one step at a time, to master one technique or skill before moving on to the next.

Speaking of mastery, I'm all about pursuing Mastery versus Overload. I first learned this concept from Peter Voogd in his book '6 Months to 6 Figures'. Too many of us flit from one technique or skill to the next without fully ingraining it into our skillset. Our attention is being pulled in so many ways with Facebook groups, forums, books, podcasts, videos, Skype study groups, Twitter, poker articles and training sites. All of these distractions are yanking at our attention strings by showing us the "shiny new thing" and hoping we follow them to it.

"Oooh, new info about 3bets? Let me watch this video."

"Wow, I should limp with pocket Aces? What's this article telling me?"

"Adding more action to my home games, I know the guys will love this chapter."

"A podcast about playing in the blinds? I'm listening to this . . . like NOW."

These shimmering baubles distract us from our real job as poker players and poker learners: developing one skill at a time until we master it before moving on to the next. We mustn't jump from 3bet concepts to new ways of playing AA to having more fun in home games to working on our blind play. This type

3

of hopscotch poker study will lead us to being semi-capable (but often pretty ignorant) in many areas . . . but masters of none.

To aid in your journey of poker mastery, this book will show you the study techniques I've developed to ingrain skills into my repertoire. These techniques have turned me into a singularly focused poker studier. I employ them to pound one skill or one play or one concept over and over into my thick skull, driving it in there permanently. This is very important because once a play is in there, it is *in* there.

It's also important to tackle each new skill with a variety of study and play techniques. I've always been a proponent of the idea that "variety is the spice of life" and incorporating new ways to approach your poker studies will keep you motivated to study *and* motivated to play for many years to come. Plus, it adds an extra level of enjoyment to your pursuit of poker mastery.

"Ain't nobody got time for that!"

Time is precious; it's our most valuable asset. The fact that it's a finite resource ought to help us to prioritize our actions and carefully choose to do what will benefit us the most.

I'm incredibly focused on *not* wasting your time with this book. Contained within are actual study techniques and mindsets that I've found extremely useful in my poker journey. I'm going to be as succinct and to-the-point as I can in relaying every piece to you.

I'm putting only things in this book that I believe will bring value to your poker journey.

We all need to work on getting more out of the hours we put into our poker play and study. By following the techniques outlined here, your efforts *and time* will be maximized around one topic, with the goal of mastering it before moving on to the next.

My objective with each chapter is that by the end of it, you will be thinking to yourself, "That's perfect, let's put it to use." If instead you say to yourself, "Ain't nobody got time for that!" then I've failed and just wasted your time with that chapter. But I promise you, that won't be the case.

How This Book Will Help You

This Book Contains All Of My Poker Study Strategies

I went all out in this book and included every strategy I use to improve my game. I left no "study stone" unturned and now you have it all. This book will teach you how to fish so you can jump in your schooner at any time and feed your family for a year. It's going to take hard work on your part, but I've laid out the tackle, hooked up your pole and pointed you in the correct direction. The rest is up to you.

Here's a breakdown of what you will learn:

Part One is about the Poker Student's Mindset. The best learners in the world are open to learning. They don't believe they know it all, and in fact, the more they learn the more they realize they don't know. Is this you? I'm sure it is because, after all, you just bought a book called *'How to Study Poker.'* I'll talk about nurturing a growth mindset and avoiding a fixed mindset. You'll learn about an incredibly important model of learning called the Process Model, and how you can utilize this on your road to poker study greatness. I will also get into some concepts I learned along the way called Purposeful Practice and Unconscious Competence. You will learn the importance of asking great questions to propel your poker studies and knowledge to new levels.

Effective learners begin with the end in mind by making a plan of attack for their studies. We will discuss that in Part Two. I will teach you to make your Poker Improvement Plan, set SMART Goals and how to focus on one thing at a time, and mastering it, before moving on to the next. I'll discuss utilizing a poker journal to record your studies and the lessons learned, as well as incorporating 30-Day Challenges to build healthy and sustainable poker habits into your arsenal of self-improvement weapons.

Part Three will hit all the techniques I've designed for in-game development of my poker skills. I will get into critical warm-up and cooldown strategies. Speaking of cooling down, you will learn how to avoid (or at least lessen) tilt by using logic statements during your time on the felt when those irksome opponents are surely getting to you. I will show you how to do my favorite on-the-felt study strategy of utilizing FOCUS Sessions to ingrain skills in your game. Of course, you are playing poker to bring in the Benjamins, so I've got to jump into volume sessions where the real money is made. And lastly I will discuss utilizing Game Tape to improve your game and catch those mistakes that hand history reviews alone just can't bring to light.

In Part Four, I will discuss all the strategies I use off the felt to improve my game. From utilizing software like PokerTracker 4 and Flopzilla for hand history reviews, to effectively learning from training videos and forums will all be discussed. And of course I will get into the number one reason I became a poker coach: to learn more and ingrain skills in my game by teaching others.

How You Learn From This Book: Follow The Action Steps

> "Action is just one of my skills."
> -Hiroyuki Sanada

With each study strategy I discuss, I follow it up with Action Steps that you can implement immediately to improve your game. Following these steps make you an active participant in your poker improvement, not just some passive observer who, if you're lucky, will learn a thing or two.

The critical thing here: follow the action steps. I designed the steps with KISS simplicity in mind to get the ball moving quickly for you (KISS is an acronym for Keep It Simple, Stupid). The action steps within this book build upon each other as the book progresses. The work you do in Part I on preparing you mentally for your journey will lead into Part II where you will begin planning your journey. The steps in Parts III and IV will build upon these as well, taking your goals and plans and turning them into action on and off the felt.

If you're not willing to take action to improve your poker game, you're just wasting your time reading this book. Put it back on the shelf, donate it to the library, delete it from your electronic book shelf, whatever.

How This Book Will Help You

I'm writing this book to help you *help yourself* to improve your game, but it's going to take action on your part to accomplish that. I guarantee that *every* action step you follow from this book will improve your game. If not . . . well, there's no "if not" because I've used every one for myself and have seen vast improvements because of them.

Action Step #1: How To Learn From Poker Strategy Books

I created a podcast episode dedicated to learning from poker books, and you must listen and learn from that before you begin Part I on the Poker Student Mindset.

Take Action:
1. Go to the show notes page for Podcast Episode #21 called 'How to Learn From Poker Strategy Books' (http://www.smartpokerstudy.com/pod21)

2. Download and listen to the episode from that page

3. Within the show notes page, get the '7 Steps to Poker Book Learning PDF' that details my 7 steps to poker book learning

4. Use the 7 Steps to get the most out of this book and every future poker book you read

* * * *

The success of your poker journey is dependent upon you taking the necessary actions to improve your game.

Kaizen & Ganbatte!

The Japanese have a word for constant and never-ending improvement: Kaizen. It's a philosophy passed down for thousands of years from warrior to warrior, and is now followed by high achievers in business, sports, technology, the arts . . . and now poker. I want you to adopt a philosophy of kaizen toward poker. In your quest for constant and never-ending improvement, I want you to ask yourself everyday:

- How can I improve my poker game today?
- What can I study that will bring me the most gains?
- What leaks do I have that I can fix immediately?

Commit to the philosophy of kaizen and seek daily improvement in your poker skills.

The Japanese have another word, ganbatte, which means good luck and succeed and get to it and do your best and "get 'er done" all rolled into one.

So on your poker journey of kaizen, I say to you, GANBATTE!

Let's get to it . . .

Part I: The Poker Student Mindset

> "You are always a student, never a master. You have to keep moving forward."
> -Conrad Hall

As a poker student, you've got to love the journey you're on. Sure, the final destination you're striving for, whether it's Main Event glory or nose-bleed cash game brilliance, would be great to make it to. But before you get there it's going to take many hours of study, grinding hands, discussing strategy with friends, watching videos and all the other things you'll do to improve your game. Ultimately, it's going to require a concentrated effort to build your skills, one upon the other, until you turn yourself into a force to be reckoned with.

In chapter 2, I'll discuss some of the characteristics that a few of today's greatest poker minds share. Don't worry if you feel you don't have these characteristics, because you can develop them within yourself with a little time and some effort.

Next in chapter 3, you'll learn about building skills to the level of unconscious competence. Following this I'll get into some theories of learning that will help us on our journey. These theories are what all my study strategies revolve around, so understanding the power they contain will make it easier for you to follow and employ the things I discuss throughout the rest of this book.

And finally I'll discuss the power of asking great questions to aid you in your poker journey. Great questions lead to great answers, and the answers you discover during your studies will aid you in every session you play.

— 2 —
Characteristics Of Great Poker Minds

> "If your mind is strong, all difficult things will become easy; if your mind is weak, all easy things will become difficult."
> - Chinese proverb

The greatest poker minds share some key characteristics. Players and coaches, like Alexander "Assassinato" Fitzgerald, James "SplitSuit" Sweeney and Chris "Moorman1" Moorman, exemplify the modern poker professional.

They demonstrate patience and perseverance with how long and hard they have worked in poker to achieve all they have. They are obviously open-minded and continue to learn and work on their game, not settling on and doggedly sticking to old ideas that once worked. They have observant and calculating minds; not just regarding the mathematics of poker, but they demonstrate their ability to adjust to changing players and table dynamics. And lastly, they are more concerned with making the best play rather than the growth of their bankroll or the results from their most recent session.

These players all see poker for what it is: a skill game that requires constant work and refinement to become a top player and to stay relevant for many years.

I would bet that Fitzgerald, Sweeney and Moorman were not born with all these characteristics. These characteristics can be developed over time and with concentrated effort. Which of us started life as a patient little kid? Nobody I know of. What about open-minded? Probably not, as evidenced by my kids always telling me "no, dad, that's not right." Great observation and calculation come via accumulated experiences while pursuing one overarching goal. And the drive for ignoring our baser, more anger-fueled, tilty instincts comes with time . . . and many struggles.

Maybe you have one or more of these characteristics already deeply ingrained in your behaviors, maybe you're missing all four. Whatever the case, understanding how they work within a great poker mind is step one to putting them in place within your own thought process.

Patient & Persevering

It takes years of dedicated study and practice to develop a solid (and eventually great) poker game; years comprised of thousands of hours spent playing the game over hundreds of thousands of hands, hours upon hours of time reviewing hands and judging the profitability of plays made, and time spent discussing poker with other like-minded individuals.

No great poker player (nor anybody who has earned lasting acclaim in business, sports, acting or any other endeavor), made it without an incredible amount of hard work. You work when you don't want to, you work when it hurts, you work when your friends are out partying. You don't do this because you're going to be successful tonight or next week or even next month. You do this because you have a force propelling you forward, and you have the patience to work harder than most now, for greater rewards down the line.

Great poker minds can persevere through any storm because they trust in the skills they have developed, and they know that in the long run their skills will prevail. They are not short-term results oriented, so they don't allow small setbacks to affect them. Yes, suckouts and terrible play getting rewarded still feels terrible, but they can quickly look beyond that at the profitable road ahead.

Your job as a poker student is to have the understanding that being a world-class player will only result from years of dedicated study and play, and putting lessons learned into action. Every journey starts with a single step . . . then another . . . and another. Thousands of "steps"—or hours spent studying and playing the game fill your journey to poker professionalism. Be positive and know that rewards come to those who dedicate themselves to the study of poker.

Action Step #2 – Patient & Persevering

At the end of your next five poker play sessions, before you look at your bankroll and count your wins or losses, rate your session play. Would you give yourself an A for great decisions, opponent reads and choices made? Or do you deserve an F for going on tilt, random button clicking and spewing chips? While results do matter in the long-term, what matters in the short-term is the quality of your play, the decisions you make and the work you're putting into improving your skills. (More on rating your play in chapter 5)

* * * *

Open-minded

The great poker mind is not set in its ways. It never says, "That's impossible," or "That would never work." It does not doggedly stick to old ideas and plays and strategies. "Times, they are a changing" is never more applicable than to the world of poker.

  This is a characteristic that I've always admired about **Alex "Assassinato" Fitzgerald**, a coach who I've interviewed twice for the podcast. He has spoken many times about his openness to new ideas, and the time and effort he dedicates to determining the profitability of any play or action at the tables. He has recounted the story of discovering that it can be profitable to open/fold a sub-10bb stack. This seemed a crazy idea at the time, but an MTT player named "Pessagno" was showing mad profits by making plays like this. Everyone dismissed him, but Alex took the time to run the numbers and found for himself that "Pessagno" was on mathematically sound footing.

  With this story, Alex demonstrated that he does something that many other players will not do: instead of dismissing a play as idiotic and reckless, he'll go home, analyze the situation, run the numbers and come to a logical conclusion for himself.

  Along with being open-minded, great poker minds are not naysayers. 2012's biggest online winner won $3.6 million, an insane amount that people thought was borderline impossible to achieve. But, even more insane is that the following year, Niklas "ragen70" Heinecker did almost double that when he won a whopping $6.3 million online. Similarly, achieving Super Nova Elite status on Pokerstars used to be the Holy Grail for grinders. It would often take the full 365 days in a year to achieve; but Andrew "azntracker" Li accomplished it in just two months back in 2011, an amazing feat.

As evidenced by these stories, Fitzgerald, Heinecker and Li are open-minded but they are also growth minded individuals. Growth minded individuals don't shy away from activities or goals because they fear failure. Quite the opposite. Growth minded individuals tackle new tasks because A) they want to test themselves and B) they are willing to fail because they know that within failure lies success. If one only attempts things that they know they can accomplish, they will never improve. Failure pushes you to learn from your mistakes, to work on necessary skills that will propel you beyond your current limitations.
"I failed my way to success."
-Thomas Edison

Your task as a poker player is to always be open to new ideas, to dissect them and run the math yourself to test the validity. Don't listen to others who tell you the "rules" of poker. The only rules in poker are what hands beat what and the order of play around the table. Other than that, you do what you want. The only limits to what you can accomplish are those you set for yourself, so keep that open-mind and strive to overcome new challenges.

Action Step #3 – Open-minded

Over your next five sessions, tag or make note of all hands where you feel your opponent made a tactical or mathematical mistake. Review the mathematics involved, the situation and the players yet to act and see if a logical explanation for how your opponent played exists.

* * * *

Always Observant & Calculating

Great poker minds are dedicated to problem solving. They use necessary tools and years of experience to find what plays may work in a given situation. A simple question a player might ask is, "How often does my cbet bluff have to work?"

The calculating player would answer with: "First you're betting 1/2 pot, so that needs to work 33% on its own (bet / total pot = %). Now let's dive deeper. Assign your opponent a range, enter it and your hole cards in Flopzilla, and determine what your opponent will call or reraise with. If your calculations say he'll fold more often than your bet sizing says it must, then you're printing money in the long run with this play. If not, what can we adjust to make this play profitable?"

A great poker mind dives deep into problems, runs the math, and uses imagination and problem solving skills to figure out how to make a situation profitable; what tweaks to ranges, hole cards and what player types can change this situation into a winning one.

I truly admire this aspect of poker pro and coach **James "Splitsuit" Sweeney**. He demonstrates his ultra-observant nature in the way he discusses poker and the questions he is always asking himself as he breaks down hands and analyzes his opponents' play. He uses these observations to devise strategies to exploit their weaknesses and tendencies. Over time, he uses these exploits on multiple opponents as he always looks for players susceptible to any given exploit.

To be ever observant and calculating, your task is to think logically in solving every problem, and to think outside of the box when necessary. If you find yourself thinking, "I can't figure out what this guy's weakness is," then it's time to dive into a hand history review on just this one opponent, view every one of his hands and his statistics, and do not give up until you find a weakness you can exploit. Everyone has a chink in the armor and it's your job to find it.

Action Step #4 – Always Observant & Calculating

Over the next five sessions, make it a goal to learn from every showdown you see. What hands did they play and how did they play them? Did their actions tell you the strength of hand they were holding? What notes could you make on the players to help you exploit them in the future?

* * * *

Strives To Make the Best Plays . . . Always

A great poker mind realizes that poker is a long-term game of profitable decision making, and the one who makes the best decision most of the time will come out a winner. If an opponent exhibits a particular weakness, then it's your job to find a way to exploit that weakness on the flop, turn or river. "There is always a way" is a common mantra of great poker minds.

I've not had the opportunity to interview Chris "Moorman1" Moorman (yet!), but through interviews I have listened to, it's plain that this is one of his outlooks on poker. As an MTT player, variance is a real issue, and Moorman1 understands this and does not let it affect him anymore. Once he considers all the factors in a given decision, he uses these to determine the correct action, then takes it, but does not regret any negative outcome. How can he? He was working with the best information at the time of the decision, he utilized his experiences to decide, and made the play he felt was most profitable. There's nothing to fault, and the outcome, whether positive or negative, is simply something to accept.

Your task is to put together all that you've learned, analyze each situation with your experiences and lessons in mind, make a decision and take action. You cannot ask for more than that from yourself. If you do this properly, you will have no regrets in your poker career.

Action Step #5 – Strive To Make The Best Plays . . . Always

Over the next five play sessions, tag or take notes on every hand where you felt you made a mistake. Review these hands, note the mistakes and why they happened, then commit yourself to not making them again. Note the lessons learned on a sticky note or in your poker journal and review these at the start of each session to remind yourself of what you're working on. (sticky notes are discussed in chapter 18 and journaling is discussed in chapter 11)

How To Study Poker

* * * *

Now that you understand the characteristics of a great poker mind, it's time to give you an understanding of how that mind works at developing skills.

— 3 —

Developing Skills To The Level Of Unconscious Competence

> "Knowledge is not skill. Knowledge plus ten thousand times is skill."
> –Shinichi Suzuki

The Four Stages of Competence was a learning theory originally developed by Noel Burch in the 1970s. It described a model for how we learn skills and their movement from a base level of Unconscious Incompetence (a beginner with very little skills) to the highest skill level of Unconscious Competence (a skilled "pro" who can apply skills without seemingly to think about them). The world's best poker players have developed a majority of their skills to this level.

Poker And The Unconscious Competence

I personally love thinking about the four levels of skill building that we all go through. Let's dive into them.

Level 1: Unconscious Incompetence

This is where we all start with our first hand of poker. We looked only at the strength of our hand, not even knowing how strong it actually was, and we decided whether to bet, call, raise or fold. At the time, we didn't even recognize there was so much more to the game than the cards we were dealt. We were so inexperienced that we didn't even know what we didn't know.

Level 2: Conscious Incompetence

At this stage, we're applying some new skills, and we are aware that there's a lot that we don't know yet. As we play and study more, we become aware of how poor our skillset is. We find ourselves in tough spot after tough spot and we have no idea how to handle it. This is screaming at us to study more to gain some skills so we can handle ourselves better at the tables.

Level 3: Conscious Competence

Now this is the stage where things are beginning to click into place. We're trying out our new skills and doing lots of practice and experimenting. We know how to use many of the skills we're working on, but we have to spend lots of concentrated effort on putting them into play. Ranging opponents, planning future streets and considering our image are all things we can do, but they don't come naturally yet and it's easy to forget to take these things into account unless we're consciously focused on them.

Level 4: Unconscious Competence

This is the stage we're striving for. As we practice our newly learned skills over and over again, they become much easier to employ and eventually come to be natural. Gut reactions take over and we have a great "feel" for the game. We don't have to purposefully range opponents because our mind is churning this out naturally as every hand progresses down the streets. We automatically see profitable spots to barrel bluff, to call down with second pair, or to fold to river aggression. This is where our A-game* lies, and it's what we have been studying and training so hard for.

*A-game is a term I first learned from Tommy Angelo in his incredible book *Elements of Poker*. It refers to playing at your most optimal level, where you're fully in-tune with the dynamics of the game and making sound, logical decisions. Sub-optimal play is called the B or C-game.

Training Skills To The Level Of Unconscious Competence

If you're like me, your goal in poker is to become one of the best. It starts with recognizing where your deficits lie and systematically working on eliminating them. You can only focus on so much at once, so this becomes a gradual process that takes time to accomplish. And, in an ever-changing dynamic game like poker,

Developing Skills To The Level Of Unconscious Competence

there are always skills to work on, new defenses and offenses to adapt into your play, and new opponents to deal with: so it's a never-ending process. If you're going to achieve in poker, you have to love the journey and be willing to do the work necessary.

The first step is finding your poker leaks. Make a list of these leaks, and put them in order of importance so you can tackle one at a time starting with the most relevant. Currently, I have a long list of 9 leaks, but here are the top 3:

1. Nonbelieving and paying off opponents too lightly
2. A lack of aggression without the nuts on the turn and especially river
3. Too much attention to my bankroll and not to the level of my play

Once you know your leaks, you can work on the specific skills needed to plug these leaks. This takes dedicated time off-the-felt to study the necessary skills, then time on-the-felt in special FOCUS sessions (discussed in chapter 15) in which you are intently concentrated on these skills and actively looking for spots to put them into play in the session. Eventually, the more you actively use the skills you're working on, the quicker they will become natural parts of your game and get developed to the level of Unconscious Competence.

For example, to plug my #1 leak of being a nonbeliever, I'm taking the following steps:

1. I'm focused on the type of player I'm up against in every session I play. I also actively consider what their every bet or raise means regarding the strength of their hand.
2. I'm striving to make a read and a note on every showdown I see of my opponents.
3. I'm reviewing hands daily where I paid off opponents who bet or raised on the turn and river

Action Step #6 – Listing The Skills You Need And Working To Improve Only One

Make a list of the 5 poker skills/areas you want to work on next.

My 5 Areas:

Example: Continuation Betting, Pre-flop Ranges, Value Betting, Outs and Odds, 3betting

Next put them in order of importance:

1. _____

2. _____

3. _____

4. _____

5. _____

Example: 1. Pre-flop Ranges 2. 3 betting 3. Outs and Odds 4. Continuation Betting 5. Value Betting

Now, begin working on improving the first skill/area on your list. When you feel you have a great working knowledge of this and can access it easily while playing, move on to the next.

* * * *

To bring the necessary skills up to the level of unconscious competence, a strong system of study and practice must be put into place. Studying and playing willy-nilly just does not cut it and you will never truly master any skills that way. You must practice with purpose and follow a logical progression of study and play to be one of the best.

— 4 —
Improving Poker Skills With Purposeful Practice

> "Practice does not make perfect. Only perfect practice makes perfect."
> -Vince Lombardi

I rigorously follow a learning concept called Purposeful Practice. With Purposeful Practice you spend your practice time on a specific skill or task to ingrain it into your skillset. If practice was all about quantity and putting time in, we would all be expert poker players by now with all the hours that we have logged on and off the felt.

We play hour after hour, and throw in some studying time watching videos and breezing through poker books. We occasionally discuss poker with friends and maybe respond to hand history reviews in forums. We sometimes get an itch to review hands from the night before, but those study sessions are often disjointed and do not have a clear direction in mind.

The way most of us play and study poker just does not build the skills the way we would like them to.

There are 4 parts to Purposeful Practice that I want you to start implementing:

1. Begin With A Clear Goal

If your current poker leak is that you call blind steals too wide or never even try to steal, then why are you studying cbetting or short stacked play or watching videos on deep tournament runs? If you want your practice to mean something, then set a specific goal for the area you want to improve.

Three examples of specific blind steal related goals could be:

1. Decrease my Call 2bet% down from 30% to 20% in the blinds

2. Increase my Attempt to Steal% from 20% up to 35%
3. Take my BB/100 hands win rate up from 2BB/100 hands in the Cutoff and the Button to 7BB/100 hands

If you're having a hard time figuring out where to devote your study time, you can use the Focusing Question presented in the incredible book by Gary Keller and Jay Papasan called *The ONE Thing.*' The question in the book is worded a little differently, but ask yourself, "What's the ONE Thing I can study right now such that by learning it everything else will be easier or unnecessary?" The answer to that question is your next study goal.

2. Plan Your Work, Work Your Plan

Now that you have a goal, it's time to plan your studies. Take some time to select videos, articles, podcasts and chapters from books that will teach you the info and skills you're missing.

Three examples of items you could study to improve your blind stealing skills:

1. Smart Poker Study podcast episodes 96, 97, 99 and 102 are all related to the Blind Stealing Minimum Effective Dose
2. Chapter 6 from Alex Fitzgerald's book *The Myth of Poker Talent*' called 'Pre-flop Raising'
3. Video 'How to Steal the Blinds in Poker' from James "Splitsuit" Sweeney and The Poker Bank YouTube channel

You will want to take notes on all you've learned as well so you can refer to them in the future. Also, do hand history reviews centered on your specific goal. In the case of improving your steals, filter your PokerTracker 4 database for your steal attempts. You need to analyze your steal attempts to figure out why they were successful or not, and determine the things you can do better in the future.

There will be much more regarding planning your studies beginning in chapter 7.

3. Challenge Yourself

This is key. I want you to challenge yourself to improve this area of your play. Put yourself in situations where you can practice what you're learning. Try to teach others what you've learned via study groups, Facebook groups and forums. You're used to playing and discussing things the way you always have, now it's your chance to push your limits and try to learn in more dynamic and impactful ways.

Three examples of ways to challenge yourself in an effort to improve your blind stealing skills:

1. Play one thirty-minute FOCUS session (discussed in chapter 15) and steal at <u>every</u> opportunity over the next five nights
2. Post one blind stealing related hand in the <u>Facebook Group</u> every day for the next five days
3. Create a training video at the end of your five days of study, teaching others what you learned about blind stealing and post it on YouTube

4. Measure Your Progress

You need to measure your progress somehow, otherwise you will not know if you're improving. You might find it a challenge quantifying your progress, but if you cannot find anything to measure, then you probably didn't set a specific enough goal. Every specific goal has a way of measuring your progress toward it.

Here are three statistics to measure your blind stealing progress. You'll want to record these before and after your time studying blind steals.

- Attempt to Steal%
- Steal Success%
- BB/100 hands win rate in the CO, BTN and SB

Action Step #7 – Utilizing Purposeful Practice

Take the #1 skill you decided to work on from the previous chapter, and run through these four parts with it. Then get started on ingraining this skill into your unconscious competence by utilizing purposeful practice.

* * *

In the next chapter I will cover some important learning concepts that when applied with purposeful practice and improving skills to the level of unconscious competence, will take our learning to new levels.

— 5 —
Utilizing The Learning Process Model

"The expert in anything was once a beginner."
-Helen Hayes

The Learning Process Model is a common-sense approach to learning. We do this naturally already in many areas of our lives. But doing it with purpose and planning our poker learning around this model will help immensely. This five part cycle, when used correctly, helps improve our skills systematically and effectively:

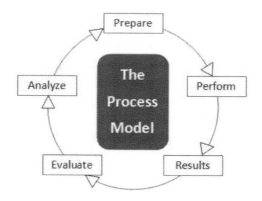

Figure 1

1. **Prepare**: This is what you do to prepare for a poker session
2. **Perform**: The session you play
3. **Results**: The outcome of your session
4. **Evaluate**: Reviewing your results after your session
5. **Analysis**: Time off-the-felt working on your game

Prepare

Preparation is key for great poker performance, and spending a few minutes to a dedicated warm-up before each session is mandatory. I discuss pre-session warm-ups in great detail in chapter 13. Pro sports players, stand-up comics, presentation speakers and actors always warm-up before they get to work. As strong poker players, we need to follow suit.

Your preparation must include a review of your current studies and area of focus. Have a one-sheet or your study notes out for your review before and during your session. Get rid of distractions (social media, television, etc.), clear up any lingering issues that might interrupt, and prepare yourself mentally for the session.

Perform

During your poker sessions, you must keep the following in mind:

- Have one area of focus for your session (or at most two areas). You ought to be working on specific skills that you're trying to put into your unconscious competence. Are you working on your 3bet game, blind stealing, focusing on playing in position only, cbetting with equity, or something else?
- Make a goal ahead of time for your session length or # of hands you'll play, and strive to hit that goal.
- Be aware of your tilt issues (add this to your warm-up routine) and be on the lookout for any triggers during your session. Have your logic statements at hand in case you need them. (more about logic statements in chapter 14)
- Don't multitask while playing (Skype, Twitter, web surfing, etc.) and just FOCUS on your play.
- Don't spend much time mid-session reviewing hands that just happened. Mark them for later review, jot a quick note then get back to the action.

Results

You don't want to be results oriented as poker is a long-term game, and wins/losses in one session don't truly matter in the long run. But every session ends with a few quantitative numbers you can record:

- $ won/lost
- # of tournaments or hands played
- Session length (time)

Evaluate

There's great value in evaluating your session beyond just the results you've achieved. This is the first opportunity you have to objectively assess the session and determine what your upcoming Analysis needs to focus on. Here are some ways to evaluate your session:

- Rate Your Play – Give yourself a rating of how well you played: A, B or C-game. Did you focus on the things you set out to do in your warm-up? Avoided tilt? Did you make great 'in the moment' decisions?
- Rate Your Session – Did variance affect your results? Did you get it in with the best hand only to lose (or maybe suck out) often?
- Post-Session Notes – Take notes for review during Analysis on anything important that you need to look further into. This can include notes you made in-session on hands as you played them, but can also include things that you later think of while reflecting on the session. Maybe you realized that one specific losing hand started to tilt you, but a quick step away from the computer put you back in the proper mindset.
- Lessons Learned – If you could go back and tell yourself three things before the session started to help you have a better session, those are your lessons learned. They are things that you need to take with you into every future session to help you play your A-game.

Analysis

This is where you get to develop your game the most. Analysis could include many ways to review your past session, dissect an opponent's play, and address weaknesses or to learn new skills (each of these topics are covered later in this book):

- Reviewing Game Tape
- Reviewing notes from the previous session
- Hand history reviews from your database
- Posting hands in forums; not just your own but responding to posts from others as well
- Watching training videos
- Working with a coach
- Reading books/articles
- Talking with poker friends about the game and issues you're facing

Action Step #8 – Working The Process Model Steps

In your next session, follow the steps outlined above. Put a warm-up in place where you review your notes and decide on a focus for the session. Play without distraction, then end your session by evaluating your play and results. Measure any quantifiables you're currently tracking and make a plan for tomorrow's analysis. The next day review your session and any aspects you want to focus on, then plan for your next session.

* * * *

Knowing how we can actively control and focus our learning (the Process Model and Purposeful Practice together) will help us all become better poker players. Another thing we can do to help ourselves work on areas of necessary improvement is to ask shrewd questions that get us thinking in new and productive ways. That's what I will discuss in the next chapter.

— 6 —

Directing Your Studies By Asking Great Questions

"The quality of your life is determined by the quality of your questions."
-Dr. John Demartini

You may not realize it, but the quality of your poker education comes from the quality of the questions you ask during your study and your play sessions. Many players don't ask any questions at all, they don't plan their studies but instead bounce from one topic to the next without a plan. They just play hand after hand, not even dreaming that a better approach to their hobby exists.

The best poker players and coaches ask plenty of great questions. This ability gets them and their students actively thinking about every situation, every opponent and every small bit of information that can aid in solid decision making.

The Most Useful Question: "Why?"

I love the question, "Why?" This type of question often puts you in someone else's shoes, to think about how they view things and how it might differ from your view.

Some great poker-related "why" questions:

- Why did the BTN check behind?
- Why did villain check-raise?
- Why is doggy543 such a nitty player?
- Why did the opponent use 5x bet sizing?
- Why does this overly aggressive player always seem to make it to the tournament chip lead?

The question, "Why?" helps you dive in and understand your opponent. Everyone has a logical reason for the things they do. And when I say logical, I mean logical to them. Your opponent might think it's terrible to raise before the flop with anything other than AA and KK. You of course don't see things this way, but you will come across many players who do. The key to exploiting your opponents is to understand their personal 'logic' for doing what they do.

For example, some players discovered long ago that their opponents chase every draw and they hate getting sucked out on. So, when they flop a strong hand on a wet board, they overbet 2xpot to get the draws to fold. The logic they are using here is, "The board is wet, I have a great hand, so I would rather win it now than get sucked out on."

This is absolutely logical to them, but maybe not to us (and definitely not to me). We would much prefer betting ¾ pot to overcharge the draws so we can get value when we flop such a strong hand. Our logic is to overcharge them, not push them off their draws.

The best time to ask these "why" questions are during hand history reviews. This is where you can take the time to dissect your opponent's choices and use their tendencies and showdown hands to help you understand the logic they are using. The more you do this off-the-felt, the more readily the answer to the "why" question will come to you when you're playing on the felt.

Turn The Tables On Yourself

"No one is dumb who is curious. The people who don't ask questions remain clueless throughout their lives."
-Neil DeGrasse Tyson

You know the phrase, "Curiosity killed the cat"? Well, that isn't true at all in poker (and in most other instances I believe). Curious people learn the most in life and they are also the ones who improve the fastest.

Curious people not only ask "why" about others, but about themselves as well. "Why" questions are perfect to help you understand your play and psychology:

Directing Your Studies By Asking Great Questions

- Why did I tilt?
- Why did I 3bet shove on the bubble with 18bb's?
- Why did I check-fold when I know that a check-raise would have likely gotten him to fold?
- Why didn't I cbet in position on that Ace high board?

Answering questions like these will help you improve your game through better understanding of yourself. If you know what tilts you, why you sometimes punt off your stack, why you don't make the scary plays, or why you miss the no-brainer plays, this knowledge will only improve your game. If you don't figure out the answers to these questions because you never ask them, you're just stifling your development.

Some Great Poker Questions To Get You Thinking

There's no end to the number of great questions we can ask to analyze our opponent or ourselves. And here are some classic examples of great questions that I've asked of myself and my students thousands of times over. These questions can be reworded many ways to fit various situations.

"What's the worst _____ they would open-raise here?"

When you're thinking about somebody's opening range, imagine it divided into four specific categories: pocket pairs, broadways, suited connectors and other hands. A great way to help you build this range is to ask which hand is the worst within each category that a specific opponent would open with.

If the worst pocket pair they would open is 88, then logically 99, TT and everything better are within the open range as well. Maybe the worst broadway they would open is QTs, then we know that KTs, ATs and QJs are openers as well.

If the worst suited-connector being opened is 86s, then every suited two-gapper up through AQs and every suited-connector 76s and better are opened with as well. And if the worst "other hand" they would open is KJo, then they are also opening KQo and AJo, but staying away from QJo.

Knowing the worst helps us determine the rest and it eliminates many hands from their range, thereby making a task like hand reading just that much easier.

"How often will they fold to a 3bet?"

This is a great question to ask before making a 3bet bluff. To know if a 3bet bluff is outright profitable (will earn the pot then and there without a fight), you compare how often they fold to the break-even percentage of the bet.

Example: A common cash game scenario: 1.5bb's in the pot from the blinds. A loose MP player opens to 4bb's, we're in the BB w/J8s. We're thinking about calling to just see the flop, but if we make a 3x 3bet to 12bb's as a bluff, what's the break-even % of that bet sizing?

$$\text{Bluff Break-even \%} = \frac{\text{Amount of Bet}}{\text{Total Pot (with bet included)}}$$

$$\frac{12}{5.5+12} = 12 / 17.5 = 68.5\%$$

Figure 2: the Break-even formula in action

The break–even math tells us our bet of 12bb's is trying to win a total pot of 17.5bb's, so 12/17.5 means our bluff bet needs to work 68.5% of the time.

Now that we know the math, let's ask again: How often will they fold to a 3bet? We can get a great indication of this in a few ways:

- If we're using a HUD online (more on HUD's in chapter 19) and we have a decent history of at least 100 hands, then

- looking at their Fold to 3bet statistic will give us a great indication of how often they fold to 3bets in the MP.
- If we're playing LIVE then hopefully we have been paying attention to how the opponent responds to 3bets. If they tend to fight back, then our 3bet bluff is less likely to succeed. If they have a super-wide opening range but a small continuation range, then they will be more likely to give up and our play is probably profitable.
- And lastly if we know nothing about the opponent that we can take advantage of, maybe we can make the 3bet here to set a tone and to learn about how they respond to them.

Many Post-flop Question To Ask

The prior two questions were related to pre-flop play (but of course they can be changed and adapted for post-flop knowledge gathering as well). There are some great post-flop questions we can ask to help us understand and exploit our opponents:

- If I bet, will my opponent fold the hands they missed?
- Does the opponent slow-play strong hands?
- What types of hands are they likely to raise here?

The questions you ask yourself, whether in-game or off-the-felt, must help you understand your opponent and to devise strategies to exploit them.

If you know that the opponent normally folds on whiffed flops, the fact that they continued to the turn indicates they somehow connected on the flop. If the opponent comes out firing but is normally a slow-player, then they likely don't have a monster hand. If you have seen villain raise with the nut flush draw and open-ended straight draws in the past, and your cbet gets raised here, then you can keep these drawing hands in their range and use this knowledge through the rest of the hand.

Practicing Your Question Asking

> "Judge a man by his questions rather than his answers."
> -Voltaire

We can all get better at asking questions that elicit deep discussion and valuable insights, but the only way to get better is to practice. Here are some of the ways we can practice asking great questions:

- Make a list of questions you can ask yourself during your hand history review study sessions. They could be math based questions, range based questions, villain player type questions, etc. Organize the list so you can come back and reference it at any time.
- Make a list of questions you can ask yourself in the middle of playing an actual hand at the table to help you dissect your opponents play on the spot.
- Make a list of questions you can ask yourself to gauge how well you're currently playing and whether you'd be better off ending your session early.
- With every training video you watch, especially with ones just released, ask the video maker to help clarify something they said.
- Hit your favorite forum and within hand history review posts, ask the original poster clarifying questions regarding the villain, maybe the range the villain could have, the poster's own range, or on anything else. Try to ask questions that will yield helpful answers to all who read the post.

Action Step #9 – Asking Great Questions On The River

Make a list of questions that you could ask yourself on the river that will help guide your river approach. Take a situation of your choice: Maybe the flush completed, the board paired, an over card came, a seemingly unimportant card came, or whatever situation

Directing Your Studies By Asking Great Questions

you want. Now, make a list of at least 3 questions to help guide your actions on the river. Think about what knowledge will help you make the value bet, the bluff bet, the check raise, the check call or the check behind correctly in this instance. Let your imagination flow as there are plenty of questions you could ask yourself to guide you to some inspired strategy.

Q1: _____

Q2: _____

Q3: _____

Q4: _____

* * * *

Now that I've discussed the mindset features of great poker students, let's get to the practical aspects to working on your game.

In Part 2, I'll give you a detailed plan, in 6 steps, to systematically discover what you want out of poker, set some goals to work towards and ultimately begin working on the necessary skills to take your game to new heights.

Part II: Plan Your Poker Journey In Six Steps

"Plan your work and work your plan."
-Napoleon Hill

You've made it this far, so it's obvious to me you're serious about your poker journey and developing yourself into a force to be reckoned with at the tables.

Poker is a long-term game and to play at the highest levels you need a plan to take you from where you are now, to where you want to be.

Your plan begins with a destination in mind. Having a solid and desirable goal to reach for, with many appropriate milestone goals along the way, will propel you to push forward and keep on keeping on when things get difficult.

Your plan needs to systematically find and improve upon your weaknesses, while building new skills into your game and honing existing skills. It needs to challenge you on a daily basis, but not be too difficult or unrealistic that you lose sight of what you need to accomplish along the way. A solid plan will guide you along your path, and will add to your enjoyment of poker as you improve in a systematic way and you see the positive results of your hard work.

This second part of the book will help you plan your studies for long-term success in poker.

The 6-stage plan outlined below is simplified as much as I could make it. I know that simple appeals to most people. Although I use the term "simple," please don't confuse this with being "easy". Poker is a complicated game full of layer upon layer of complex strategy, and ruled by people who spend their entire lives studying the game.

I originally created this plan for myself to follow, and I use it to great effect, as I am sure you will also. I made the plan with the KISS principle in mind, but it's as thorough as it needs to be to propel you onward and upward through your journey.

— 7 —

Step 1. Determine Where You Want Poker To Take You

> "If you can dream it you can do it."
> -Walt Disney

Every journey needs a destination. Where you want to go determines what you need to do to get there. Are you looking to become a poker pro? Want to just make a few hundred extra dollars a month while keeping your job? An aspiring cash game professional will have a far different journey than an MTT weekend warrior will.

Action Step #10 – Finding Your Poker Destination

Answer these questions for yourself to help you determine where you want poker to take you:

Why do I play poker?

At what level of play (buy-in or stakes) will I feel I have achieved something great by reaching it?

Do I want to play poker full-time, or just use it as a profitable part-time endeavor?

* * * *

Your answers to these questions will guide you to your desired destination. Once you know where you want to go, you need to create some SMART Goals to strive for in your poker play and studies.

— 8 —
Step 2. Set SMART Poker Goals

> "Set your goals high and don't stop till you get there."
> -Bo Jackson

SMART is a popular acronym used by many different sectors in relation to goal setting (I didn't choose it just because it fits my brand name). Peter Drucker first mentioned the acronym back in 1954 in a book called *'The Practice of Management.'* It stands the test of time because it's so incredibly intuitive, easy to remember and works exceptionally well.

SMART goals require a lot of thought to put together and are designed to aid the creator in achieving them. A SMART goal is defined as Specific, Measurable, Achievable, Relevant and Timebound.

We will break down each part of the SMART acronym by examining a common goal that many MTT players make at least once in their lifetime: playing in the WSOP Main Event:

> I will play in next year's WSOP $10,000 Main Event by saving $835 per month from my poker bankroll over the next 12 months.

Specific–The "S" in SMART

SMART goals must be Specific; they define exactly what you intend to accomplish in clear and simple language.

The Main Event goal above is a very specific goal, detailing exactly which event will be played and when that will happen. It also includes what must be done every month until then in order to afford that hefty $10,000 buy-in.

Besides a financial goal like this, in poker you can make goals for mental game improvement, the number of hands played, hours played, tourneys played, increasing the maximum number

Step 2. Set SMART Poker Goals

of tables when multi-tabling, study goals, forum post goals, videos watched goals . . . anything goes. As long as your goals help you achieve what you're hoping to get out of your poker journey, I'm all for them.

Measureable–The "M" in SMART

SMART goals must be Measurable. If you cannot measure them, how do you know you've achieved anything? And, measurable goals allow you to break it into milestones to make the pursuit of each much more possible in your mind.

With the Main Event goal, you know exactly how much money you have to save per month for 12 months to have the full buy-in. This can even be broken down further into weekly savings goals if that would help. Hitting shorter-term weekly goals may help to keep you motivated as this is 52 quick short-term wins as opposed to twelve long-term wins over the course of the year. As the months (or weeks) pass, you know exactly how close you are to achieving your goal as that envelope under your pillow gets fatter and fatter.

Achievable–The "A" in SMART

Smart goals must be Achievable and not impossible; you ought to feel stretched and challenged by the goal, but it can't be so obviously out of reach that you're doomed from the start. You need the knowledge, skills or abilities to achieve the goal, or be able to plan how you're going to gain those things. Ultimately, achievable goals motivate, impossible goals derail progress or prevent you from even starting.

This goal of saving for and playing in the $10,000 Main Event is definitely achievable. It all depends on your current income, your ability to increase your income or your ability to withdraw from your bankroll.

Relevant–The "R" in SMART

SMART goals are Relevant and matter to you and those around you. If your goal is to make millions of dollars playing in poker tournaments, then striving to play in the Main Event is a no brainer. It's the most prestigious tournament with one of the biggest prize pools every year.

If you're a cash game player on the other hand, you would be better off skipping it and targeting something else as a goal. Also, if your family and friends are down with your goal, it's much easier to achieve with their support. If your wife or husband is always complaining about your poker trips and tournament losses, then heading to the Main Event might not be the best idea. Maybe making a goal of strengthening that relationship or turning them into a poker player would be better for you and your sanity.

Time-bound–The "T" in SMART

SMART goals are Time-bound. Any task expands to fit the time allotted to it, so a goal without an end date could take years to attain. Deadlines add a sense of urgency and push you to accomplish your goal.

Setting this Main Event goal twelve months away puts a perfect deadline on it and gives at least a small sense of urgency. Twelve months can seem like a long way off, and staying motivated for an entire year can be difficult. I'll share a few tricks that help me deal with long time frames.

Goal Achieving Insights

Through my time making and achieving SMART poker goals (and some failures thrown in as well), I've developed some insights that help me stay motivated and focused.

1. Break It Up – Goals of longer than a 90-day duration are more prone to suffer from procrastination and de-motivation. Regular feedback is better, as quick wins keep us propelled, focused and motivated. So like we did with saving the full $10,000 buy-in, break any goal you make into smaller milestone goals. Short-term milestones are great for lots of feedback. You can also take a "ramping-up" approach to your goals. The Main Event goal here was broken up into saving $835 per month. What if that's out of your current abilities? Maybe start with $400 this month, and as you build your skills target an additional $80 in savings each subsequent month. $400 this month becomes $480 the next, $560 following that, and so on until the final two months are

Step 2. Set SMART Poker Goals

$1,200, making your total saved for the year $10,000. You started off slow, ramped up, and charged forward at the end to take you to your goal.

2. Make Support Goals – Just setting one big SMART goal for the year does not work well for me. I always create some support goals whose achievement help propel me toward the big goal. For the Main Event example, $835 per month may be beyond your current skills. To have monthly winnings like this, what skill acquisition goals or time spent playing goals or mental game improvement goals could help you earn more at the tables? Whatever would help to boost your poker income to achieve your goal must be a part of the support goals you set.

3. Map Out What Needs to Happen – What skills will you have to improve to achieve your goals? Which leaks currently cost you money? You need to know what to work on, so make an honest assessment of your current game, and make a list of leaks to fix. Then, systematically tackle this list one at a time. Gear all of your study toward fixing these leaks or adding new skills to your repertoire. If you don't know which skills you may need to add, I recommend you look into my Poker's Minimum Effective Dose series of podcasts (http://www.smartpokerstudy.com/pod87). In this series I lay out the top 10 skills that every player MUST KNOW in order to be a complete poker player. Start with MED #1 and work your way through them all.

4. Get Others Involved – Do you need to enlist the help of a coach? Maybe start a study group? Goals are always more easily achieved if you have a team of people working on them. Don't do this on your own, enlist a team and help each other.

5. Accountability – Personal accountability is a great motivator, so tell others about your goals. Choose people who will hold you to the fire. Whether it's a best friend, poker bud, significant other or your Aunt Susie, tell someone who will ask you about your progress and keep you on track. It's beneficial if your accountability partner is someone whom you feel you will have let down if you don't achieve your goal. Plus, it's great if your

accountability partner has some stake in your goal and would also gain if you succeed (like a husband or wife). Public displays like sharing goals with your family, friends and poker study buddies are great as well because it feels like all eyes are on us so we work extra hard to achieve.

6. Periodic Assessment – Each quarter, month or week you must assess your progress. Are you on track to meet your goal? Are your milestone goals getting hit? You may have to reassess your goals and make some changes, or buckle down and work even harder to achieve them.

To help you in your goal setting, I've made available The SMART Poker Goal Setting PDF. You can download your own copy by going to http://www.smartpokerstudy.com/HTSPsmartgoalsPDF.

Action Step #11 – Setting One Smart Goal & Two Support Goals

Now that you have determined where you want poker to take you, it's time to set a SMART goal that will get you there. Follow the aspects of SMART as outlined above to make your goal and write it here:

SMART Goal:

What makes my goal Specific?

Measureable?

Achievable?

Relevant?

Time-bound?

Step 2. Set SMART Poker Goals

Create two support goals as well that will give you a leg up on achieving your big goal.

SMART Support Goal #1:

SMART Support Goal #2:

Share your goals with somebody who will hold your feet to the fire, will push you to achieve them and also stand to gain from your accomplishments.
Accountability partner:

* * * *

— 9 —
Step 3. Choose The Necessary Skills That Will Get You There

"Acknowledging you have areas to work on is not an admission of failure; it is an admission that you have more potential."
-Carrie Cheadle

So you know where you want to go, and you've set some goals to propel you on your journey. The next step is to figure out the skills you need to add or improve to get you there. You want to start with skills that will have the biggest effect on your game, the ones which mastering first will propel you the furthest.

The 80/20 Principle

I consistently use the 80/20 Principle to help me determine what I must study next. The principle states that 80% of your results come from 20% of your efforts. This is a "provable, predictable certainty of nature" according to Keller and Papasan in 'The ONE Thing.' This means we need to focus on a small number of things that will produce most of our results.

We must not allow ourselves to become overly busy or focused on things that do not move the needle much. If studying open raising ranges will yield 20% more profits and affect every street of play, and studying river value bets will yield 3% more and only come into effect on the river, which is the smarter focus?

Yep, I know your answer to this and you are correct!

We need to focus on the things that will give us the biggest gains in our skillset, and be productive doing just those things. Once we figure out what truly matters to us, we need to keep asking what matters most until only one thing remains, and that's what we need to do.

Step 3. Choose The Necessary Skills That Will Get You There

Back To The Focusing Question

Remember that list of skills to work on that you made at the end of chapter 3 within that chapter's action step? Here are the example skills I listed within that chapter's Action Step:

1. Pre-flop Ranges
2. 3betting
3. Outs and Odds
4. Continuation Betting
5. Value Betting

Let's say this is your list, and you've determined that pre-flop ranges are the most important topic to tackle first. Perfect topic, but it's pretty broad. Which aspect of pre-flop ranges is most important to begin with? Within this topic there are:

- Open raising ranges
- 3bet ranges, both value and bluffs
- Calling ranges
- Steal ranges
- 4bet+ ranges

So where to begin? Which of these aspects of "Pre-flop Ranges" is the one to target first? If you don't already know where to begin, this is the perfect time to bring back the Focusing Question:

> "What's the ONE Thing I can study right now such that by learning it everything else will be easier or unnecessary?"

This one simple question, if asked with a clear goal in mind, will lead us to the ONE Thing that we need to study RIGHT NOW before all the others. That ONE Thing will make it easier or unnecessary to do other things. It's the first step in a process of steps to achieving our goals.

In my mind, the order of importance within these aspects of pre-flop ranges is pretty clear:

1. Open raising ranges – because as strong poker players this is how we most often enter pots, as the pre-flop open raiser
2. Steal ranges – stealing blinds and antes is incredibly important in poker and is a natural follow-up to creating open raising ranges
3. 3bet ranges, both value and bluffs – with aggression being such a prevalent part of today's games, we need to understand this aspect to pre-flop poker which happens quite frequently
4. Calling ranges – this necessarily follows the first three items here as hands worth calling are weaker than your 3bet hands but better than your 3bet bluffing hands
5. 4bet+ ranges – this is the action that happens the most infrequently pre-flop, so it necessarily takes up the final spot on the list

By using the Focusing Question this way, you break down the important initial area or skill into more manageable pieces that build upon each other. This creates the roadmap of your poker studies.

I mentioned earlier that we need to keep asking what matters until only one thing remains, and that's what we need to work on. We must continue to ask ourselves the Focusing Question to get as granular as we can, so that we can find an ultra-specific focus for our studies.

So, within the aspect of open raising ranges, there are even more sub-aspects to this (in order of importance):

1. Early Position (EP) open raising range
2. Middle Position (MP) open raising range
3. Cutoff (CO) open raising range
4. Button (BTN) open raising range
5. Blind open raising range

Now we have an even better initial area to begin our studies on open raising ranges. Ranges get wider as position gets later, so starting with the EP range will allow us to simply add

Step 3. Choose The Necessary Skills That Will Get You There

hands when we devise our MP range, then add even more hands in the CO and more on the BTN. The blinds are a slightly different beast to tame, so taking what we have learned about the other positions will inform our choices here. This progression of building upon prior studies is well characterized by the Domino Effect.

The Domino Effect

The Domino Effect (as discussed in 'The ONE Thing' by Gary Keller and Jay Papasan) states that a domino can knock over another domino 50% bigger than itself. Then that domino knocks over another bigger one, then another and another. Well, this has amazing implications for improving your poker game. You're not going to topple the humongous domino of "poker mastery" quickly or easily. But if you start with small dominos, work on building your game in smart incremental steps and choose specific topics that build upon each other, over time you will eventually get to the point where you can topple that huge mountain-sized domino that you're striving for.

So, by looking at the examples I've been discussing, after you topple that first domino of opening ranges, what's the next? According to the example list, it's Stealing Ranges. We can now drill into that using the principles discussed here, to get granular and find our next topic of study that will yield the biggest results.

We will continue this way, knocking over one domino after another, in our progression to poker mastery and ultimately reaching our end goal.

Action Step #12 – Using The 80/20 Principle, The Focusing Question And The Domino Effect

Take the #1 item from that list you created back at the end of chapter 3 within the action step and break it down until you're left with the most important aspect to begin your studies with immediately. Use the 80/20 Principle and the Focusing Question to drill down, then list the importance of these granular topics using the Domino Effect.

#1 Topic:

80/20 Principle: What area of study will yield the biggest within that topic?

Focusing Question: What skill, once mastered, will make everything else easier or unnecessary?

Domino Effect: Each subsequent area of study will build upon the previous.
Granular Topic of Study #1:

Granular Topic of Study #2:

Granular Topic of Study #3:

* * * *

Now that we know how to narrow our studies to the most important skills to work on right now, we can create a plan for self-improvement of our game.

— 10 —

Step 4. Create A Weekly Plan For Improving Your Game

> "Failing to plan is planning to fail."
> -Allen Lakein

I know you're dedicated to improving your game, so you must spend one hour at the beginning of every week planning your week of study. You must write down your plan and commit to it.

I created a Weekly Poker Study Plan to help in your planning. You can download your own copy of this PDF by going to http://www.smartpokerstudy.com/HTSPweeklystudyplan.

Download the plan, print it, and then follow along with the steps below. I've also included the weekly plan at the end of this chapter.

As I discuss each part of your weekly plan, I'll approach the process through the eyes of someone wanting to improve their 3bet game.

Committing To A Singular Weekly Theme

Having one particular theme for an entire week will give you singular focus and allow you the time to explore it in detail. This dedication to one area will help ingrain the concepts into your game as you study it from a variety of angles.

Something very unproductive happens when you flutter from one topic to the next without any clear direction. If you watch a 3bet video today, filter for hands where you folded to the cbet tomorrow and then read Jonathan Little's book *'Secrets of Professional Tournament Poker'* the next day, you will just succeed in overloading your brain with too many disparate concepts. This does not promote mastery with any of them.

With all the poker content out there in the form of podcasts, books, videos, articles and coaching, it's too easy to get distracted by the "shiny new thing" that comes across your Twitter or FB feed or wherever you get your poker strategy fix. The way I get around this is to pick one thing to study for a week at a time, I study that topic one hour every day, and I ignore everything else that comes my way.

The concept of learning that I follow this way is called Mastery versus Overload (first mentioned back in chapter 1). Tackling one topic each week, over the course of a year, will allow you to fully develop skills in 52 different areas (as opposed to bouncing around and studying 150 throughout the year). Imagine what your game would be like a year from now if you spent one week each on 52 different skills; each skill building upon the last until you increase your level of play well beyond your current ability.

Your goal with poker learning is to master one thing at a time before moving on to the next, and selecting a different theme each week will help in this regard.

So, we can continue on to the "hypothesis" step with the idea that our theme for the week is 3betting.

Creating Hypotheses

For any theme you're studying, create some hypotheses ahead of time concerning what you think you will learn. Hypotheses are educated guesses about the conclusions you will draw or findings you will discover from studying the theme you've selected. These hypotheses will guide your study and push you to find the answers to questions raised or to verify if your initial, unstudied thoughts on the matter are accurate.

Hypothesis Examples for a 3betting Theme: If you don't have that much experience with 3betting, here are some hypotheses you may come up with as you ponder the week of study ahead:

- I believe I'm way too tight when it comes to 3betting. I seldom 3bet bluff, so I probably have to add that play into my pre-flop game.
- I think it's probably okay to 3bet with any pocket pair in the blinds vs a steal attempt.
- It would be best if I never 4bet bluff versus tight 3bettors.

Step 4. Create A Weekly Plan For Improving Your Game

- I bet the pros 3bet with every hand under the sun. I need to research this to see how the top players construct their 3bet ranges.
- I need to add more 3bet-related statistics to my HUD and popups.

Tracking Quantifiables

What metrics will you keep track of before and after this week's study that will help gauge your progress and your understanding of the theme?

Here are some great metrics that you must track if you're studying 3bets:

- BB/100 hands win rate as the 3bettor and as the caller
- Pre-flop 3bet% by position
- Fold to Pre-flop 3bet After Raise
- Pre-flop Squeeze%
- 3bet Steal%
- Fold to Pre-flop 3bet after Steal%

We cannot improve what we don't track, so keeping an eye on these statistics as you learn more about 3betting will tell you if your studies are affecting your play.

Choosing Your Study Methods & Content

There are plenty of ways to study the theme of your choice each week. Beyond PokerTracker 4 and Flopzilla for hand history reviews, there's almost too much poker strategy content available just waiting to be consumed.

If you're going to review videos, there are dozens of videos on every topic on YouTube and within all those pay-for-play training sites. What about books? There are volumes upon volumes of books out there. And articles, podcasts and forums? There are plenty of those as well.

With so many things to possibly study, it pays to make a list of the items you want to study this week. Do this on Sunday as you plan the week ahead. Spend a little time on Google and within your favorite training sites searching for quality content from different content producers.

PRO TIP: Utilize different content producers. You must consume differing viewpoints on any topic you're studying. Splitsuit has his thoughts, as does Andrew Brokos and Pete "Carroters" Clarke. By hearing how each of them view the topic of 3betting for example, you can pick and choose what makes the most sense to you. You can then take those ideas, perhaps something different from each content producer, and fuse them into your own view on 3bets.

After a quick Google and YouTube search for "poker 3bet" here's a list of four interesting and education items perfectly suited for a week of 3bet research:

1. Article: The 3-Bet | How To 3-Bet Light By Greg Walker on ThePokerBank.com
2. Article: Breaking Down the Three-Bet by Daniel Skolovy on PokerListings.com
3. Video: How to 3-bet for Value Pre-flop by Poker Quick Plays on YouTube
4. Video: How To Build An Un-Exploitable 3-Bet Range IP by Poker Strategy on YouTube

With this list in your plan, you'll hit a different piece of 3betting content each day, and you'll watch/read/listen to it with a critical ear. And, an important aspect you MUST DO is to take notes on all you learn. You can do it in a physical journal, Word document or Evernote. Whatever works for you, just do it.

Planning Day By Day – Combining Daily Studies With A Daily In-game Focus

Next, we look at our week and decide day by day how we will spend our one hour of study. You will probably find yourself repeating many of the same modalities day after day, especially if you love videos and hate reading books, or if you love going through your database but hate everything else. But, I urge you to switch things up and learn from different sources all the time.

Step 4. Create A Weekly Plan For Improving Your Game

This helps to keep your mind nimble and active as you're consuming content in different ways. It also helps to alleviate boredom.

FAQ: "How often should I study?"

Most poker players will find great benefit in studying 1 hour per day. This is very easy to fit into anybody's schedule, and at 1 hour per day, I guarantee you're putting in more study time than 95% of your opponents.

> **When you are not practicing, someone else is.**
> **When you meet him, he will win.**
> **-Martial Arts Proverb**

When it comes to study, you have to have some self-awareness of your current skills. If you know you need much more work to be an effective and profitable player, study more than 1 hour per day. If you're very experienced and hardly ever find yourself in tough spots and are making great money at your stakes, you will be fine studying less often.

I don't recommend cramming all your studies into one day per week. There have been numerous scientific studies that show cramming for tests helps for just that one test, but it doesn't promote long-term recall of the material studied. Do daily study sessions to give your brain time to make connections between the things you study.

Also, if you love to study, then do more! If you don't love it, force yourself to do the one hour of study per day until it becomes a habit. Use only the techniques you enjoy or can at least tolerate if study is tough for you.

If you think you can't fit in 1 hour per day of study, here's what I recommend: stop binging shows on Netflix every day, utilize your lunch break, wake up one hour earlier, go to bed one hour later, sneak it in at work, etc. If your poker improvement is truly important to you, you'll find a way to get it done.

If you still think you can't find one hour to study every day, here's the $10,000 question: if I offered you $10,000 to study one hour per day every day this week, could you find a way to do it? If the answer is yes, then just do it. (Of course, I'm not offering you $10,000.)

* * * *

For the four pieces of 3betting content mentioned above, I would recommend studying an article on Monday and Wednesday, the videos on Tuesday and Thursday, and finding a fifth thing for Friday. You can mix in some database analysis as well as some game tape reviews or even some forum hand posting on different days.

PRO TIP: Block your study time. Make an appointment with yourself for 1 hour (at least) of study time daily, and stick to your one hour commitment. Put it in your calendar (Google, Outlook, etc.) and treat this as a scheduled business meeting, Christmas dinner at mom's house, or a dinner date with a supermodel. You would not skip any of those, so put this on your daily calendar and don't miss it.

The second part of this step is having an in-game focus as you play each daily session. This is your chance to actively put into practice the things you're learning each day. In every session of poker play, you will strive to use the tactics and strategies that you worked on off-the-felt, hopefully the same ones you studied earlier that day.

In-game Focus Examples for a 3betting Theme: Actively search for spots to bluff 3bet. You studied it earlier in the day and devised strategies for pulling them off more frequently and profitably. Put those strategies into action and see if your off-the-felt conclusions translate into on-the-felt profitable plays. You need to tag all hands with PT4 where you put your strategies into action so you can review them the following day.

Taking Notes & Reflection

I quickly discussed it earlier, but note taking is extremely important. This is your chance to put your thoughts and findings down on paper to help you remember them and it also allows you to easily go back and familiarize yourself with whatever you studied. We all know the importance of note taking back from our days at university because that's what meant the difference

Step 4. Create A Weekly Plan For Improving Your Game

between failing and passing many a test. So, take jam-packed, actionable notes.

And, at the end of your week of study and focused play, it's a perfect time to reflect on all you've learned. I recommend trying to condense your notes into a one-sheet summary of all your most important findings. This one-sheet will contain the biggest lessons learned, which would be all the things you wish you could tell yourself if you could go back to the start of your full week of study.

Action Step #13 – Planning Your Work And Working Your Plan

Download and use the Weekly Poker Study Plan for the next week starting Sunday. Spend an hour on Sunday morning planning your entire week of study and play. Pick study materials ahead of time, break it up over the week and take note on everything you learn. Work on using what you learned earlier that day in your play sessions, and make sure to time block your study sessions to ensure they get done.

* * * *

I know you understand the importance of having a plan for poker improvement. Now it's up to you to strategically improve your game through planning, commitment and follow-through. In the next chapter I will discuss tracking your progress to chart your growth.

How To Study Poker
SPS Weekly Poker Study Plan

Weekly Theme _____

Week of _____

Hypotheses (what I think I'll learn from this week of study):
1.
_____
2.
_____
3.
_____
4.
_____

Quantifiables (trackable statistics that indicate any progress made):

1. _____ Starting % _____ Ending % _____

2. _____ Starting % _____ Ending % _____

3. _____ Starting % _____ Ending % _____

4. _____ Starting % _____ Ending % _____

5. _____ Starting % _____ Ending % _____

6. _____ Starting % _____ Ending % _____

Step 4. Create A Weekly Plan For Improving Your Game

Study Methods & Content (HH reviews/forums/video/game tape, etc., & pre-selected poker content):
Methods Preferred:

Online/Book Content:

Day 1
Topic Studied: _____
Study Method: _____
Content: _____
In-game Focus: _____
Play Duration: _____
Rate Play: _____

Day 2
Topic Studied: _____
Study Method: _____
Content: _____
In-game Focus: _____
Play Duration: _____
Rate Play: _____

Day 3
Topic Studied: _____
Study Method: _____
Content: _____
In-game Focus: _____
Play Duration: _____
Rate Play: _____

Day 4
Topic Studied: _____
Study Method: _____
Content: _____
In-game Focus: _____
Play Duration: _____
Rate Play: _____

Day 5 _____

Day 6 _____

How To Study Poker

Topic Studied:	_____	Topic Studied:	_____
Study Method:	_____	Study Method:	_____
Content:	_____	Content:	_____
In-game Focus:	_____	In-game Focus:	_____
Play Duration:	_____	Play Duration:	_____
Rate Play:	_____	Rate Play:	_____

Notes, Reflection & Summary (What are the most important things you learned? How did you apply them to your game? What would you go back and tell yourself at the beginning of the week if you could?

_____

_____

_____

_____

_____

_____

_____

_____

_____

— 11 —
Step 5. Keep A Journal & Track Your Progress

> "Write what should not be forgotten."
> -Isabel Allende

Keeping a poker journal is the best way to systematically work on your poker skills. Your journal is an active engagement tool and will be by your side before, after and during every study and play session you take part in.

With a poker journal you can:

- Keep track of your leaks and what you have done regarding them
- Track your study and play time
- Track your tilt issues
- Form or crystalize your thoughts on poker plays/strategies
- Reacquaint yourself to past topics you've studied
- Put your thoughts down on paper for posterity or to use in the future as a book, blog post, strategy article or when coaching students

There was a time when I didn't keep a poker journal. Back then, if you had asked me, "How's your poker study going?" I would have probably given some sort of noncommittal grunt.

But the full truth is that I felt lost in my studies. I was like most players and bounced from topic to topic, never stopping to think how I could study and improve my skills in a logical and systematic way. I could not remember all I learned, nor implement the concepts consistently. I know that I was so overloaded with different strategies and techniques that nothing was being cemented within my skillset.

It was like this for many years and improving was a constant struggle as I was always pulled in different directions by the "shiny new thing."

I needed some way to organize my thoughts and be able to go back to them and try to make sense of things. I had to find a way to put my ideas together to devise new strategy insights, a way to track my progress and to systematically go from topic to topic while giving myself time to employ strategies learned.

That's when I discovered journaling. Actually, it was the book by Hal Elrod called *The Miracle Morning* that led me to begin journaling in an effort to improve my poker game.

How Journaling Helps

Journaling can help you improve mental clarity

You need a way to put together disparate thoughts, going from a jumbled mass of ideas in your head to creating effective strategies and gaining insights into poker. By putting these things down on paper you can look at them from a distance and gain a better understanding of your overall game, how you're improving and where you're heading.

You also need to keep track of your weekly studies, and journaling is very effective in tracking what you've studied and what you intend to study down the road.

Journaling can help you combine ideas for effective new strategies

Maybe last week was spent on studying Opening Ranges and Raised First In statistics, and now this week you're working on cbetting and cbet statistics. By combining these two topics, Raised First In and Cbet, you may think of some ideas and strategies that you can use to exploit your opponents.

For example, you might color code these the same so you're more likely to notice them on your HUD, or you will make a note in your warm-up each day to look for players with both statistics being high, and these are perfect opponents to raise their cbet or to float them and take it away on the turn.

Step 5. Keep A Journal & Track Your Progress

Journaling can help you find and address issues that you were unaware of

When you notice something popping up more than once in your journal, it's an obvious thing to follow up on. Maybe over the past three weeks you found the following entry four times, "How do I play against these crazy pot size donk bets by fish on the flop?" With several mentions of this particular issue, it's something you must get to the bottom of.

Journaling can help you track your progress

By tracking your progress, you can see your ups and downs in poker, where you're making strides or where you're falling behind. Maybe tilt is an issue, and though you've been working on it, you play your C-game 2 out of every 5 sessions. By purposely tracking things like this in your journal, you know it's accurate. If you just rely on how you think you've been playing, it's easy to deceive yourself into thinking you only play your C-game maybe once every 10 days.

What Do I write?

Now that is completely up to you, but the more thorough and organized your notes are, the better. I'm not going to give you exact instructions on how to keep a journal on your studies, as I trust you will figure out what works for you over time.

But regarding what to write, I do have a few suggestions to help you get started. First, you will use your journal before and after each play and study session. You will also take notes during your sessions of anything worth of noting. Divide your journal into two sections; one for your play sessions and the other for study sessions.

Play Sessions

With play sessions, you want to write about what went well or poorly during the session, what your focus was going into it, what might have baffled you and any mistakes made and the reasons why. You want to record your warm-up process so you can repeat it next time or make improvements to it. (more on warm-ups in chapter 13) You want to rate your session and any tilt you experienced with notes on why it happened.

To start your journaling, begin by answering these six questions that your poker coach might ask you:

- What did you do for a warm-up?
- What strategy focus did you have?
- What mistakes did you make?
- What spots baffled you?
- How extreme was any tilt and why did it occur?
- How would you rate this session and why? (pass/fail, letter grade, # out of 10)

Study Sessions

With study session entries, you want to keep track of what specific topics or themes you're working on. I would love to see you have a list of weaknesses that you're systematically addressing. Write the Focusing Question in BIG FONT at the top of your first page to get you thinking along those lines.

Again, to begin your entry, answer the following six questions that your poker coach might ask you:

- What concept did you study?
- How did you study it?
- What lessons did you learn?
- What questions do you still have?
- What further topics do you need to study to fully grasp this concept?
- What outside help do you need?

If your journal answers each of these, then you're keeping excellent track of your studies and you will have a great document to refer to in the future to refresh your studies. You may even be able to use it as your first poker strategy book!

Step 5. Keep A Journal & Track Your Progress

Logistics And Journal Reviews

Utilizing an electronic journal is great, especially for recording your study sessions. These are easily searchable, "copy and pasteable" (for your future book), and will never run out of space. You don't have to go fancy, just a simple Word document will do.

I also want you to have a system in place for reviewing and reflecting upon your past week's entries. So, every Sunday morning as you drink your coffee, revisit the prior week. Try to look at your entries with 'fresh eyes' and see what nuggets of wisdom and understanding you can glean from them.

Do these weekly reviews before you spend an hour planning your next week's studies. The lessons learned from the prior week will inform your upcoming week, and make your next plan better.

Now the last thing I want to say to those not sure if they want to employ journaling: **don't think, just do.** Grab an empty notebook just lying around and commit to journaling for one week. See where it takes you and how you enjoy it. I guarantee it will not hurt your game.

To help you out, I have a Poker Journal Questions PDF that will help guide you to optimal journaling. You can download the pdf by going to http://www.smartpokerstudy.com/HTSPjournalquestions.

Action Step #14 – Begin Journaling

I said it once, but I will say it again: don't think, just do. Grab that unused journal sitting there on your bookshelf and get started. Begin with writing down your focus for your next play session, then record how well the session went and whether you kept your focus. Did you tilt? Did you make logically sound decisions? Were you distracted by Skype or Netflix? The more you journal, the better you will get and the more benefit you will receive. So, get started today.

* * * *

For some people, journaling feels foreign, uncomfortable and is therefore a tough habit to incorporate into their life. If this is the case for you, then utilizing a 30-day Journaling Challenge could be the answer. More on that in the next chapter.

— 12 —
Step 6. Build Strong Poker Play And Study Habits

> "We are what we repeatedly do. Excellence then, is not an act, but a habit."
> – Aristotle

What is a habit? It's something we repeatedly do and we find it hard to quit doing it. Maybe we find it fun, compelling, rewarding . . . maybe it's an addiction or a compulsion. In this chapter we'll focus on building beneficial habits using 30-Day Challenges.

I will be up front with you; thirty days is generally not enough to build a habit. Research has found that on average it takes sixty-six days to build a new habit (from a study called "How are habits formed: Modelling habit formation in the real world" by Authors Lally, Van Jaarsveld, Potts, and Wardle first published in July 2009.) We can start with a 30-day challenge though, and if it's enjoyable and we're gaining lots of value from it, we can just repeat for another thirty days. This also solves the problem of starting something new for 66 days feeling like an insurmountable task (especially if we're not sure we will enjoy it).

As poker players, we would all love to adopt healthy poker habits that lead us to greater gains in skill and profits. Here is a list of Poker 30-Day Challenges I've accomplished or that I will do for this year:

- Daily Warm-up before session (I'm sometimes overeager and fire up tables too soon)
- Post a hand on a poker forum each day
- Give up alcohol
- Read a poker strategy article each day
- Record thirty minutes of game tape each day and watch it the following day

- Write a detailed blog post about one HUD statistic each day; broken down 8 ways from Sunday
- Create a Twitch account and broadcast a session every day

5 Steps to Fulfilling 30 Day Challenges

As we go through the steps below, we will look at them with the idea of building a habit of daily study for one hour per day.

1. Have A Goal

It helps having a SMART goal in mind to propel you through the 30-day challenge. Just wanting to adopt a healthy habit might be enough to complete all thirty days, but having a SMART goal to accomplish in the process will make it more meaningful to you and will incentivize you to push through the tough days.

SMART Goal: By the end of 30 days I want to have a strong grasp of SNG play so in the final five days of the challenge my ROI will be 20% over 100 SNG's.

2. Make A Plan

Now that our SMART goal is set, we can make a plan for what we will study in the thirty days to attain it.

So, for a SNG study plan, we can study each of the following topics for four days each: Early Stage play, Mid-stage play, Late Stage play, On the Bubble play, In the Money play, ICM considerations and Heads-up play. That's seven topics over twenty-eight days. We can spend the two additional days on studying common SNG leaks, and there you have it, a full thirty days' worth of SNG topics to study to make us a stronger player.

3. Start Small

If this habit is new or tough for you, then start small. If you've never studied more than two hours per week, how can you expect to do *seven* hours in a week? We can follow the same plan for the SNG topics to study, but start day one with twenty minutes and add two minutes per day to our study time. On day twenty-one we'll be at sixty minutes. We have effectively upped our tolerance a full 3x.

4. Plan For Failure

If the challenge is tough but worth doing, plan for failure. As just mentioned, it will be difficult to go from two hours of study to seven per week. Likely, we will skip a day for some reason. But if that does happen, it's not over. DON'T QUIT! This is not "all or nothing" or "go big or go home." This challenge is worth completing, so get back on that horse and complete it.

If we do miss a day, we can fall back on Plan B: the following day we wake up 30 minutes earlier than normal and do 30 minutes of study. Then later we follow our normal study plan for the day. Back on track! Just create that Plan B ahead of time in case you need it.

5. Create a Reward

We're much more likely to succeed if we dangle a killer carrot out in front of us as a reward for completing the 30 days. Sometimes the intrinsic reward of knowing you accomplished a task just isn't enough to push us through the tough parts.

Maybe there is something special we have our eye on; a beautiful new bow tie, or a new 40-pound bow and arrow, or The Arrow seasons 1-4 on DVD. Whatever it is, it's a great item to now reward yourself with for completing the 30-day challenge and improving your poker skills.

Action Step #15 – Start A 30-Day Challenge

Set your own poker-related 30-day challenge. Follow the five steps outlined above and dedicate the next thirty days to instilling a new and healthy poker habit in your life.

To help you out, you can download a copy of my 30-Day Challenge Tracker by going to http://www.smartpokerstudy.com/HTSP30daytracker

* * * *

This concludes Part II on your poker journey. You have enough now to logically plan your poker future and set yourself up to go as far as you want this journey to take you. In the next two parts of this book, I will give you on-the-felt and off-the-felt strategies to work on strengthening your poker game.

Part III: Study Techniques For In-Game Work

"Practice hard, play hard, be hard to beat."
-author unknown

Many players separate their skill acquisition and study time from their playing time. Well, it's completely possible to do both together and that's what we will dive into in Part III. There are plenty of ways you can work to improve your game as you're playing poker, you just need to learn how to do it.

— 13 —
Poker Session Warm-ups & Cooldowns

"Proper planning and preparation prevents poor performance."
-Stephen Keague

I'm sure you know the phrase, "Set yourself up for success." By incorporating a thoughtful warm-up before each session, you will do just that and be more likely to have a profitable A-Game session.

Every sport or game requires warming up:

- Long-distance runners warm up their muscles with a few laps.
- NASCAR drivers always visualize every twist and turn of a race before the starter flag is waved.
- Football teams go over the plays on the sidelines while they are warming up their bodies.
- Basketball players are taking shot after shot pregame, getting their muscle memory fired up.

Poker players don't often incorporate warm-ups into their games, and their play suffers for it. Warm-ups get you in a positive poker mindset, focus you on your current strategy training, prepare you to handle the inevitable beats without tilting and allow you to play longer sessions more effectively.

Simple And Effective 3-5 Minute Poker Warm-up

I keep my warm-up nice and simple with only 2 steps that takes anywhere from 3-5 minutes.

How To Study Poker

1. Ditch the Distractions – They suck your attention away from the session you're playing and the skills you're trying to put into play. You know what the major culprits are: Internet browsers, phones, social media, television, sports, podcasts, training videos, alcohol, other people, etc.

2. Whip Out the Journal and Answer the Following:

Why am I playing tonight?

- This question is to get you focused on your current SMART goal. Everything you do related to poker must be in service of achieving this goal. Is this session bringing you one step closer?

Am I currently in A, B or C game mentality?
- Ideally, you're in A-game mindset mode. If not, figure out why and try to get into it. If not, are you in a positive mental state to play a session?

What's my one strategy focus tonight?
- This is your focus for the session. Are you working on your 3bet game? Not paying off opponents? Practicing and getting used to new open-raising charts?

What's my 5-minute Question tonight?
- I use a Tabata timer set for 5 minute intervals, and when it goes off I ask myself one question every five minutes throughout the session. Something like, "Is this table still profitable?" or "Who is my profit target at this table?" or "What playing style does each opponent have at this table?" This exercise keeps me focused on the game and on the one skill or important aspect I'm working on.

Logic Statements
- I write down at least two logic statements that I need to keep in mind to help me deal with the inevitable tilt-inducing situations that seem to come with every session I play (more about logic statements with examples in chapter 14).

Poker Session Warm-ups & Cooldowns

Pro Tip: include one part of your HUD to focus on, as well as a "Combo Stat" to look for each session. These are statistics that when paired together give you insights into opponent weaknesses. For example, if their Flop Cbet = 30%, and their Fold to Flop Cbet = 65%, you know you've found a very "flop honest" player. Use this info to take away a majority of flops from them.

The warm-up prepares you for the session ahead. Conversely, the cooldown is where we decompress and gather our thoughts after the session.

Quick & Easy Cooldown

Like warm-ups, often poker players overlook cooldowns.

Assess your play most accurately by evaluating it immediately after your session with it fresh in your mind. You don't want to think about how you're playing *while* you're playing as that often puts you too much into your head and throws you off your game mid-session. Think of a golfer whose thoughts on the mechanics of his swing mess up his swing.

I try not to think about the money won or lost in the session as the short-term results don't matter. This is one of my leaks as mentioned earlier so it's something I'm trying to force myself to do (ignore results).

Within my journal, usually on the same page where I wrote my warm-up, I answer the following 3 questions:

What was my level of play?
- Was I in A, B, or C-game mode throughout the session? If I wasn't in A-game mode, what was the reason? Is this something I can work on for future sessions?

If I could go back to the beginning of the session and tell myself one thing, what would that be?
- This is my lesson learned for the session. By the end of every session, I usually learn something new. The lesson learned might be an understanding of a certain opponent, some new insight into statistics or strategic plays, or an insight into my own game or mental game. No matter what, there's always something to take away from every session played.

Did I experience any type of tilt?
- If so, what was it, how strong was it and what set me off? What lesson can I take away from this for improved future sessions?

Action Step #16 – Do Your First Warm-up And Cooldown

I know you saw this one coming. You don't even need a journal to do this. Just ditch the distractions, then whip out a piece of paper and answer the five questions as your warm-up.

After the session, do a quick reflection on the session as your cooldown and answer the three questions above.

* * * *

14

Control Tilt With Logic Statements

"Anger is only one letter short of danger."
-Eleanor Roosevelt

For the longest time I allowed tilt to take over far too many of my sessions at the poker tables. At least once out of every three sessions I played, negative variance, bad beats, suckouts, fish getting the better of me and overly aggressive opponents would put me on tilt.

It was funny, I would expect all sorts of non-tilty things to occur in every session:

- I expected I would be dealt AA at some point
- I expected to find an opportunity to 3bet bluff the LAG opener
- I expected to hit my flopped flush draw occasionally
Those were all fine and dandy, but what I didn't see coming was the tilt-inducing situations:
- I didn't see the runner-runner flush coming that would put me on tilt
- I didn't anticipate my opponent catching the flush when I flopped my straight, which of course would send me on tilt
- I didn't expect the fish at the table to be holding 84o to beat my KQs, which would dumbfound me and send me on tilt as well.

We know that the variance in poker is something you can't control, but what you can control is how you react to the negative variance you will eventually encounter at the tables. An attitude of acceptance toward variance will help you deal with the inevitable ups and downs that come with playing poker.

Expecting the variance and beats that will inevitably come will allow you to plan for it, and having a plan in place will make it easier to lessen the tilt you experience from it. My plan to deal with tilt-inducing situations is to always have logic statements at the ready.

Logic Statements

In my pre-session warm-up, I always have two or three logic statements I say to myself in preparation for the session. These carefully crafted statements inject logic into my thinking and to help me get past negative emotions.

One of my favorite logic statements that I constantly use and apply to almost every session of poker is:

> **"Control what you can control, maggot, and let everything else take a flying fuck at you. And if you must go down, go down with your guns blazing."**
> **-Cort from Stephen King's 'Wizard and Glass'**

While playing a session, something may happen that could make me have thoughts like:

- "That's so unfair! My AA should never lose to JTo."
- "Damn it, sucked out on again by this FISH!"
- "I don't care what it takes, I'm getting my money back from this guy."

The statements above are illogical, and I know they will just lead to me going on full-blown tilt. Logic statements get me beyond these negative thoughts and get me back to thinking correctly about poker and the negative variance I can encounter.

Types Of Tilt And Helpful Logic Statements

Jared Tendler in his book 'The Mental Game of Poker' lists 7 different types of tilt, and we all are susceptible to at least one of these (I'm affected by three in particular: running bad tilt, injustice tilt and entitlement tilt). Here are the types of tilt Tendler discusses and some poker logic statements I created (some are adapted from ones in his book) that you can use for each. Keeping helpful logic statements ready at hand during your play sessions provides a simple and effective way to help maintain an A-game mindset.

Running Bad Tilt

This is a form of accumulated tilt that gets worse over time. When you're 2-3 buy-ins down, it might not be so terrible. But after a few days or weeks of running bad and being down double-digits in buy-ins, one can go on tilt super quickly at the drop of hat. These statements help me:

- I can't control how I run in the short-term, it's only the long term and making great decisions now that matters.
- I'm a long-term winner, so I know I will get past this downswing soon and get back to my winning ways.

Injustice Tilt

When you cannot believe "these crappy players" keep beating you no matter what they play with or how strong your starting hand is, you're suffering from injustice tilt. You feel ultra-unlucky, and you're being dealt bad beat after bad beat, and your terrible opponents keep getting rewarded for poor play. These statements help me:

- I can handle negative variance, as I know it has to occur to make poker profitable.
- I can only control how I play, not the cards dealt to me. As long as I'm making logical decisions, I can stomach what comes of the plays I make and those of my opponents.

Entitlement Tilt

You suffer from entitlement tilt if you believe you deserve to win because you're a better player: that your studying, hard work or discipline means you must win over all your opponents. Statements to help:

- My studying, skills and discipline will win for me in the long run.
- Weak players need to win occasionally to make this a profitable pursuit.

Hate-Losing Tilt

If you hate to lose, try to win every hand or think you deserve to win every MTT or SNG you play, hate-losing tilt is a problem of yours. You cannot accept variance or the occasional losing session, and anything other than variance in your favor is unacceptable. These logic statements will help:

- Negative variance only affects me if I let it. I'm committed to playing my best regardless of what the cards bring me.
- It is necessary that poor players suck out on occasion, as this keeps them in the game and makes poker profitable.

Mistake Tilt

We're all learning to become better poker players, and of course mistakes are a part of learning. If you let mistakes get to you and throw you into your C-game, then you know this is one of your tilt issues. Statements to help:

- Don't cry over spilled milk. Mistakes happen, just tag the hand and review your mistake later.
- Losing does not equal poor play.

Revenge Tilt

When you feel the need to get back at one single player who beat you, and it consumes you and blinds you to the hands you play or the position you're in against him, then revenge tilt is an issue. Statements to help:

- Focus on the easiest targets at the table, and only play in profitable situations versus them.

- Don't rationalize poor play in order to get into hands with a perfect target. It's important to always strive to make profitable decisions.

Desperation Tilt

If you find yourself chasing lost money by buying-in to more games or moving up in stakes to win your money back, then you've hit desperation tilt. This form of tilt can lead to incredible bankroll downswings, so it's key to tackle if you suffer from it. Logic statement:

- As soon as I hit my stop loss for the session, I will end it. No exceptions.

Action Step #17 – Find Your Tilt Type And Prepare With Logic Statements

You know that you will face tilty situations within your next few poker sessions, so start planning for it now.

Decide which form(s) of tilt you suffer from the most and write down three logic statements to have at the ready. Review them in your warm-up, then plan to use them in-session when the inevitable occurs.

* * * *

— 15 —

FOCUS Sessions: Building Skills While Playing

"The successful warrior is the average man, with laser-like focus."
-Bruce Lee

For many players, when they start a session of poker, they just load up the usual number of tables and get to work. When doing this, they often go on auto pilot and the new ideas and techniques they are working on don't get put into play. 12-tabling does not allow your mind the time to actively think deeply about each situation you're involved in. Putting new plays or skills into action, ones outside your unconscious competence, is near impossible when multi-tabling.

Incorporate FOCUS Sessions in your play schedule to embed skills into your unconscious competence. FOCUS Sessions give you more time to think through your actions.

What Is A FOCUS Session?

FOCUS Sessions are your opportunity to take more time to make decisions by cutting down the number of tables you play. FOCUS is an acronym for Follow One Course Until Success. I learned this from fellow podcaster John Lee Dumas. For best results, limit FOCUS sessions to just one or two tables for up to one hour of play. After the hour, take a break and assess the session. Need continued FOCUS? Get back to it, otherwise, quit for the day or begin a normal volume session, which I discuss in the next chapter.

With each FOCUS Session, put into action your newly developing skills, one at a time. You're trying to train one specific skill into your unconscious competence, and that takes dedicated effort with solid focus to do so.

Playing a minimum number of tables gives you enough time to look for spots to incorporate the new skills and techniques into your repertoire. The extra time allows you to weigh more factors in your decisions such as player statistics and reads, table dynamics and situational factors (first round of tourney, on the bubble, etc.).

Example: You're working on your cbet game, something you've not studied yet, and you're trying to break out of your fit-or-fold way of playing. This being the case, you probably need to pay utmost attention to the following:

- Who will be your likely opponents on the flop
- Their flop/turn statistics (Fold to Cbet, Cbet, Raise Cbet, etc.)
- Have a plan in place for the turn and river before you bet, raise or call on the flop
- Table/tourney conditions and how they may affect your opponent's play

Follow These Five Steps For Effective Poker FOCUS Sessions

Proper Warm-up

Keep your study notes out in front of you and incorporate reviewing your notes in your warm-up. This will keep your FOCUS top of mind and you can refer to your notes as you play your session.

Limit The Number Of Tables

Play only one or two tables maximum. You may feel you can handle more, and I'm sure you can, but your focus will be pulled in too many directions for it to be considered a true FOCUS session.

Record Your Session

Create your own game tape (chapter 17) and speak your thought process aloud clearly for each decision made. Make sure you're paying particular attention to situations in which you can employ the skill you're working on. Speaking through all of those situations will help you later dissect your thought process on implementing the new skill.

Keep Your Journal Handy

Have your journal close to record necessary observations and hands that you want to review. You will also want to record situations that baffle you for later analysis, or ideas for future areas of study.

Conduct A Post-session Review

You will want to conduct your post-session review within the following twenty-four hours. Don't do it immediately after your session, though (but do a quick cooldown with reflection as previously discussed). You need some time away from the session so you can look at your plays more objectively. Review your notes, any marked hands in your poker tracking software, and watch your game tape. Create a list of things to target in your next FOCUS Session.

PRO TIP: Use a tick sheet during FOCUS Sessions to help you stay focused on the task at hand. I discuss how to use them in chapter 18.

I incorporate one FOCUS Session for every three Volume Sessions I put in. This cuts down my volume a little bit, but I know that this extra time spent "sharpening the saw" is improving my game. Additionally, I sometimes do combo sessions where thirty minutes is a FOCUS Session then the second half is a Volume Session.

Action Step #18 – Build A Skill To Unconscious Competence Using FOCUS Sessions

Make your next session a FOCUS session. Choose a skill you're working on, open two tables maximum, and look for spots to put it to use. Consider all the factors surrounding your new skill and diligently use it at opportune times. Take notes on what you're learning and record the session.

Make sure to review the entire game tape the following day to judge how well you employed your new skill. Take notes on what was acceptable and what went poorly. Then hold another FOCUS session utilizing the lessons learned so far to ingrain your new skill even further into your game and skillset.

* * * *

I guarantee that you will see results when you start implementing FOCUS Sessions. By putting new skills in your unconscious competence you will experience:

- More achievements on the felt with an increased sense of understanding and poker knowledge
- The ability to put into play lots of skills
- A skyrocketing of your ROI and hourly rates

— 16 —

Volume Sessions: Learning While Earning

"There are three ingredients in the good life: learning, earning and yearning."
-Christopher Morley

We all love playing Volume Sessions. Getting a cup of tea and a water, doing a 5 minute warm-up, starting the software, loading up lots of tables (currently I play 4-6 tables) and getting to work.

Volume Sessions are the fun times when we get to make money by putting our skills to the test and pitting ourselves against our rivals. I always start feeling strong and energized to take on the competition and I have developed some techniques to keep myself going during my 1-2 hour volume sessions.

Why Poker Volume Sessions Are Necessary

Volume Sessions are the key to building our bankrolls, earning a poker income and gaining more experience in the game. To achieve your bankroll or poker income goals, you need to play a minimum number of hands or tournaments.

Example: You're a SNG grinder and want to increase your bankroll by $1,500 to start playing the next level with a 200 buy-in bankroll. If you're a $.55/SNG winner, you need to play 2,727 SNG's to earn that $1,500. If you only play 15 SNG's per day, that will take you 182 days. Half a year!!! But if you can (sanely) play 45 SNG's per day, then you'll have your $1,500 in 60 days. See the difference playing more can make?

Caution: Volume Goals can be detrimental to your progress. In the above example, some players can increase their play from 15 SNG's per day to 45 without any ill effects. But this 3x increase can take its toll. Forcing yourself to play more games (or hands if you're a cash game player) like this can be quite a struggle, and can lead to lots of C-game, sub-optimal play. Be careful before implementing an increase to your volume and do so gradually, assessing the level of your play as you go.

Volume Sessions Test The Skills In Our Unconscious Competence.

We spend so much time studying and working on our game off-the-felt. We also practice putting new strategies into play through FOCUS Sessions. But Volume Sessions are where we get to see how much we have actually learned and are able to access at the height of our in-game stress. Paying attention and noting hands during Volume Sessions will tell you what gaps exist in your skills.

Imagine you've recently spent a week working on pre-flop 3bets. If over the next five sessions you experience no confusion in any 3bet spot and make plays instantly knowing that they are correct, then you've probably (I hesitate to say "officially") put 3betting pre-flop into your unconscious competence. If, on the other hand, during those five sessions you had numerous 3bet issues and situations that confused you, then you know you still need to work on it through study and FOCUS Sessions.

Volume Sessions Allow Us To See How We Are Managing Tilt Issues

Throughout a Volume Session you will encounter many situations that might tilt you; suckouts, fish waking up with AA, the Internet connection gives out, etc. One of your jobs as a poker player is to not blow your money because tilt takes away your ability to think logically. Fixing tilt problems is critical, and Volume Sessions are the most likely place for tilt issues to emerge. Please refer back to chapter 14 for a discussion of tilt and ways to overcome it.

Start fixing your tilt. Through your next five Volume Sessions, take note of spots that lead to tilt. What emotions did you feel before tilt set in? What situation(s) brought it about? Work on taking a deep breath, injecting logic by saying one of your prepared logic statements and not letting the tilt take over your mind.

How To Get The Most Out Of Volume Sessions

Set a Goal

Setting a goal for the number of hands or tourneys played or an amount of earnings you want to achieve in the session will help you put in the necessary volume. Track this session by session to give you further motivation to check off that box every night. You may even want to set a stop-loss goal for your volume sessions if you tend towards desperation tilt and you feel forced to chase lost money.

Do Not Go Overboard on the Number of Tables

Find what works for you and run with it. Use common sense when trying to play more tables, and if you start to get overwhelmed by the number of decisions you have to make, you know that is your threshold. Remember, the more tables you have the more money you can make, but there is a point of diminishing returns when your ROI starts to decrease due to the added stress the extra tables put on your mind.

Warm-ups

For every session that you play, you want to start with a quick and simple 3-5 minute warm-up.

Game Tape

I highly recommend that you record thirty minutes of game tape for each session of play, regardless of whether it's a Volume Session or a FOCUS Session. Recording your game tape triggers your self-talk and helps you gauge your state of mind. Are you shutting up and just clicking buttons, or are you thinking through your actions and can easily verbalize them? Game tape is discussed in great detail in the next chapter.

Volume Sessions: Learning While Earning

Timer and Music

One of the best things that I've incorporated to help me stay focused throughout the session is to have my Tabata timer go off every 5 minutes (get any of the free smartphone apps available). If I don't have a specific 5-minute Question chambered from the warm-up, I will use this timer as a reminder to me that says: "Hey, guy, are you thinking through your actions? . . . don't robotically click buttons . . . have a reason for each action you take . . . you're not feeling angry, are you?"

I will often listen to music as I play, but I keep it turned down quite low and I choose music I'm very familiar with or that has a steady beat that keeps me moving and grooving.

Take Breaks

Intense multi-tabling over too much time can dampen your spirits and drain your energy. Be smart and take breaks at least every hour. It's easy to do if you're a cash player (sit out for 5-10 minutes) or an MTT player (the mandatory hourly break at :55 after every hour). But as an SNG player, you need to force yourself to stop loading more tables after about 45 minutes.

Regardless of what you play, when you do break, make sure you step away from the computer and focus on something else for a bit of time (fold laundry, cook some ramen, play Madden, whatever).

Action Step #19 – Playing More Thoughtful Volume Sessions

Before you jump on the maximum number of tables for your next volume session, plan ahead to get the most out of it. Treat it like the money making opportunity it is; not like the boredom-avoiding hand-after-hand volume fest that many players think of it as.

* * * *

Do what I outlined here: set a goal, choose a sensible number of tables, incorporate a warm-up and game tape, play your favorite music and plan your breaks to keep your mind fresh.

I generally play 3 Volume Sessions for every 1 FOCUS Session. This helps me keep my volume up, while still allowing some dedicated time to 'sharpen the saw' in the FOCUS Sessions.

— 17 —

Game Tape: The Most Underutilized Yet Beneficial Study Technique

"Watching tape is key. I basically watch every game. It's the only way to break down your opponents."
-Tony Parker

Game Tape is the most beneficial yet underutilized self-study tool available to you, and it's the one technique the pros (and your opponents) wish you didn't use.

Game tape is one of my favorite modes of in-game study and I use it constantly. Occasionally, my thought process can become clouded because I am forced to make multiple snap decisions on many tables. During a hand history review once, I actually found myself folding AA in the big blind versus one open raiser. The only explanation I came up with for this is that my attention was probably being pulled in so many directions at once, so I missed this hand. I timed out and the software folded it.

You must incorporate watching your own Game Tape in your study sessions. This valuable strategy for improvement can lead to great insights that hand history reviews alone will not give you. Game Tape forces you to be honest in your assessment of your poker play and skills. When you watch yourself play, you become privy to some of your biggest poker leaks and can make plans to address them.

People in all walks of life watch themselves at work to improve their performance and skills: sports players and coaches, presentation speakers, stand-up comedians and actors just to name a few. They look for mistakes made by themselves or their opponents, technical or message issues, and audience reactions. Once they find an area needing improvement, they work on it to make their next outing better than the last one.

As poker players, we can utilize game tape to do the same. Some areas where game tape has helped me:

- Leak Detecting – I found an MTT bet sizing issue once where I would open the pot for 2.5bb's with my strong hands, and only open to 2.25bb's with my weaker pocket pairs and suited connectors.
- Mistake Catching – there have been multiple instances of seeing myself miss obvious steal and resteal spots because I didn't take the time to look at my opponent's statistics or to fully consider the situation at the time.
- Concentration Slipping – I always speak through my actions while recording game tape, and I know when my concentration starts to slip is when I shut my mouth and fail to speak through each decision made. I've actually seen myself open Skype on the screen over my tables before and start communicating with others.
- Tilt Preventing – I've seen myself on-screen getting sucked out on, and then yelling into my microphone some obscenity directed at my opponent. These instances helped me realize what put me on tilt so I can plan for healthier ways to deal with and prevent it in the future.
- Opponent Dissection – This is an extremely important aspect to utilizing game tape. As I play poker I'm mostly concentrated on my play and the current hand in action. Because of this, I often miss the action on other tables and fail to see obvious mistakes my opponents make. By catching more of their mistakes, I have additional insights into how I can exploit them in future hands.

Five Steps To Implementing Game Tape

Game tape is a very simple study method to employ. Don't let a lack of experience in recording video hinder you from instituting such a valuable technique.

Here are the quick and easy steps to utilizing game tape.

Game Tape: The Most Underutilized Yet Beneficial Study Technique

1) Set-up And Test A Screen Capture Program

Get a screen capture program of your liking. I use Open Broadcaster Software. It's free to download and easy to set up and use.

Once you download the software, run a YouTube search on "open broadcaster software tutorial." A plethora of videos popup and within 10 minutes you can have the software up and running.

PRO TIP: Get a decent set of headphones with a microphone to use to record your thought process as you play. Your first set does not have to be an expensive pair, just a cheap pair of Logitech headphones will do. Don't use the microphone built into your computer as that quality will just tend to annoy you during your game tape reviews.

Play your next session and record from the start for 10 minutes. Once you stop the recording, just continue playing and finish out your normal session.

PRO TIP: Speak your thoughts out loud as you play to aid in later review as this will help dissect your play and your mindset at the time.

Watch your video afterward and just observe yourself in action. This is a test and it's your first time doing this so just sit there and try to absorb whatever insights you can.

PRO TIP: If the sound effects settings on your software are too high, you may have to go into the software and adjust it so you're not annoyed by them in your game tape reviews.

2) Record An Actual Session

Now it's time to record a full session.

Continue to speak your thoughts out loud as you play. This self-talk is crucial to getting the most out of your game tape.

At first, you will find yourself often just shutting up while you work out a hand in your head. Playing while speaking your thoughts is just another muscle to develop. With time you will be speaking for a full thirty minutes and beyond. Talking through your plays helps to work out your thoughts and come to profitable decisions.

How To Study Poker

>**PRO TIP:** Just record 30 minutes of your session because you will review your Game Tape at least twice. It's hard to learn all you can from the Game Tape after watching it just once.

After thirty minutes, turn the recorder off (or just set the record length to thirty minutes) and finish out your session normally. But, please continue to use self-talk as you play.

>**PRO TIP:** Record both Volume Sessions and FOCUS Sessions.

3) First Review–Focus On Your Play

At a later date (not directly after your session as it's still too fresh in your mind) you will watch your Game Tape with your poker journal open and your focus on your play. Take detailed notes on mistakes, and corrective actions for the future. Use "!" when a mistake gets repeated. An example note you may take:

> "I didn't cbet versus OOP* opponent with 75%+ fold to cbet!! I need to remember to look at an opponent's fold to cbet every time I'm in a hand."

In this entry, you've seen the mistake three times during the Game Tape, once for the observation itself and 2 more times hence the (!!).

*OOP is "out of position", IP is "in position".

Take notes on the things that occur to you that need further study or follow-up, and commit to that follow up. Taking notes is more beneficial when you pursue them. Sample note:

> "I have trouble when opponents make pot-sized donk bets on the flop. What are they doing this with? Follow up on this and study with hand history reviews, forums and articles."

Pay attention to the thought process that you verbalize in the video. What are you doing at the points when you're obviously thinking clearly and making rational decisions? You might hear yourself say something like, "This guy's opening 35% and his fold to 3bet is 68%. I can 3bet steal here with ATC" and then in the video you see yourself profitably making the 3bet bluff. Other times the steal might not work, but that becomes an opportunity to review your play and determine if you made a mistake.

Game Tape: The Most Underutilized Yet Beneficial Study Technique

What are you doing at the points where your thought process seems muddled or you're just not speaking at all? For me, my speaking becomes unclear and stilted when I face a difficult decision for a lot of chips or my tournament life. I take note of those spots and make sure to review them to figure out why I'm having such trouble. Sample note:

"I clam up when faced with a 3bet from the blinds when I've got a mediocre hand. I will make a 4bet/fold chart so I can refer to that each time to free my brain space for other decisions."

Make sure to have PokerTracker 4 and Flopzilla open to analyze hands as you pause and resume the video repeatedly. Do not let this opportunity to focus on the math and statistical analysis pass you by.

4) Second Review–Focus On Your Opponents

Because there's so much to gain from watching your Game Tape, you will need to watch it a second time with an emphasis on your opponents. If your tables are tiled, you can focus on a few opponents and just watch how they play, looking for what hands they showdown, bet sizing, timing tells and other indications of weakness.

You might want to focus on other regulars at the tables, or the fish, or the super-aggressive players who always seem to build nice stacks. You're looking for ways to exploit your opponents. If one opponent always min-bets the flop and turn and checks back the river with second pair or worse, you've now learned you can raise that opponent's min-bets on the flop or turn to take it away from their weak showdown hand.

Open your poker tracking software and make notes on players when you find specific weaknesses. A player note example: bobby2345–will call down 1/2pot bets on ftr w/2nd pair– VALUE BET RELENTLESSLY BUT DON'T BLUFF

5) Prepare For Your Next Session

Take your notes from two (or more) review sessions and plan how you will implement any game changes. Whether you incorporate them into your next FOCUS Session or Volume Session, you need to put them in your warm-up so they will at least be top of mind.

Record the next session, and see if you implemented the changes, plays or skills that you had intended to before the session began.

Rinse and repeat steps 2-5 for incredible poker breakthroughs!

Ongoing Game Tape Utilization

Make reviewing Game Tape a common study tactic (1-2 times weekly). This has been an integral part of improving my game. It helps me focus on the skills I'm trying to ingrain in my unconscious competence, and I've found that using self-talk before I act certainly helps me not make as many boneheaded plays.

As you play and speak through your actions, you will sometimes catch yourself saying something crazy. "I don't know what to do here? Well, I guess I can shove and hope he folds . . . " Hearing yourself verbalize terrible reasoning like this can snap you out of it and prevent you from making some brain dead plays (like betting without reason in this example).

Not only will you learn a lot from Game Tape, but you may find you've got a knack for commentating. You could be the next Mike Sexton!

Action Step #20 – Record Your First Game Tape Session

Follow the steps outlined above and record your first session tonight! Download OBS and just fire it up. Record tonight, watch tomorrow and learn from it.

* * * *

Part IV: Study Techniques For Off-The-Felt Work

> "You cannot fail without your consent. You cannot succeed without your participation."
> -Rob Thomas

The key to productive and efficient off-the-felt work on your game is Active Participation. As you've seen from all the step-by-step instruction and the Action Steps presented in this book, I'm trying to get you to actively participate in your studies.

Too many poker players skip the step of using what they learn off-the-felt. Some players do the bare minimum; watch videos and read books, but never put any new skills to use. Other players use poker software just superficially; run hand histories without trying to learn from their mistakes or only utilize it for the in-game HUD. Even more own great software like Flopzilla but never whip it out to improve their understanding of their game.

I don't want you to be one of those ineffectual, passive learning players.

In Part IV, I dive into the many off-the-felt study techniques I employ to improve my game. I know from firsthand experience that the many years of my passively consuming poker content got me nowhere. When I became an active participant, my skills saw improvement and I began to win more. I want to see the same thing for you.

— 18 —

Utilizing 25 Different (And Simple) Study Techniques

> **"Anyone who has never made a mistake has never tried anything new."**
> -Albert Einstein

Poker players don't realize that they can simplify their studies by employing many study techniques from their youth.

Here's a list of 25 simple but effective study techniques. Some are discussed elsewhere in this book, and others are just mentioned here. I'll give a quick explanation of each as well as a poker application in which you can use the technique to further your poker education.

This is by far NOT a complete list of every technique available. If you know of any others not on the list, jot them down here to give yourself more ways in which you can work to improve your skills.

1. Study Everyday
   - That's what school was all about. Daily reinforcement of principles and lessons learned help them to "stick" in your mind.
   - Poker Application: One hour of study per day around one theme each week.
2. Spread Out Your Studies
   - In high school and university we rotated classes, hitting five or six each day. We didn't spend all of Monday on history, and Tuesday all on math and so on. Breaking it up relieves boredom as well as allows the mind to digest what was learned.
   - Poker Application: Spread your studies throughout the week as a daily activity. Don't try to put in marathon study sessions one day a week.

Utilizing 25 Different (And Simple) Study Techniques

3. Schedule Your Studies
   - Putting study time on your calendar makes it more important, more likely to get done and can go a long way to establishing daily study as a habit.
   - Poker Application: Wake up one hour earlier and hit the books every day before work.
4. Journal Your Studies
   - Journaling about what you study helps you to crystallize your thoughts on the subject and allows for connections between ideas studied. It's also a great record keeper and helps to re-familiarize yourself with concepts learned. And, you can turn it into a book one day.
   - Poker Application: Take note of every video/article/book you study with URL's so you can revisit quickly.
5. Sticky Notes
   - This is a concept I learned about from Alex "Assassinato" Fitzgerald. Whatever strategy or skill you're studying off the felt, put the most relevant and actionable information on a sticky note for quick reference during your play sessions. Attach this sticky note to the monitor in front of you.
   - Poker Application: Maybe you're developing your 3bet bluffing ranges and you've finally settled on using A2s–A5s plus T9s and 98s for your 3bet bluffs. Let's say you've also decided to 3bet bluff vs anybody in the CO, BTN or SB with a Raise First In (RFI) HUD statistic of 30% or greater. Perfect. Write all of that on a sticky note and when you encounter all of these factors in a situation, then this is your opportunity to attempt the 3bet bluff.
6. Use Apps on Your Smartphone
   - The smartphone in your pocket is an invaluable resource for learning poker as well as helping to record your play or to keep notes.
   - Poker Application: Using Evernote for LIVE reads on players; Float the Turn app for push/shove tournament charts; a Tabata timer to force yourself to take breaks or to re-focus on the table.

How To Study Poker

7. Study Groups
   - We all spent twelve+ years studying with others to learn math, reading, writing, the state capitals and all the president's names, so why not do the same with poker? Poker learning mustn't be an individual effort, and I'd go so far as to say not a single one of the best players in the world studied on their own.
   - Poker Application: Join a Skype study group, Facebook group, hometown poker group or just find one like-minded individual and begin learning with them. Your growth will help their growth and vice versa. Be selective who you let in, though. You want growth minded individuals with positive outlooks, not close-minded and negative people.
8. Mind Maps
   - A mind map is a visual representation that organizes information. It shows the relationships between a central theme and its constituent parts.

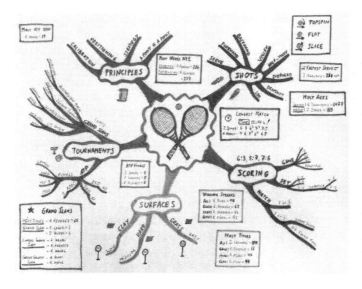

Figure 3: Tennis Mind Map from Wikipedia; https://en.wikipedia.org/wiki/Mind_map

   - Poker Application: Creating a mind map to help you understand the relationships between HUD statistics like

Utilizing 25 Different (And Simple) Study Techniques

VPIP and PFR (Voluntarily Put Money in the Pot and Pre-flop Raise). Or even making a mind map for an entire book to help you recall the most important and applicable aspects.

9. An Environment That Promotes Study
   - There isn't much to do in a classroom other than the work the teacher assigns, and libraries are perfect for the same thing as there's just a lot of books, desks and chairs around. Limit the distractions, and your studies are more likely to get done and be fruitful uses of your time.
   - Poker Application: Smartphone in airplane mode, TV turned off and tell your family you love them but you need some alone time with your poker books.
10. Have A Study Goal
    - Back in school you studied with a goal in mind: acing the test or passing the class or impressing your friends. Goals keep you motivated and push you to continue when things get boring or tough.
    - Poker Application: You want to understand a certain opponent at your tables because they always seem to soul read you. So, you decide to devote the next three sessions to understanding him and finding ways to exploit his frequency issues.
11. Note Taking
    - Back in university I took more notes than I dreamt possible. Every class I attended, every book I read and every study session I went to required me to take notes if I was ever going to remember it all. And, I finally learned in my third year to re-write all of my notes as this helped to cement the concepts learned even better in my brain.
    - Poker Application: Never study or play a session without some form of note pad in front of you. I guarantee every note you take helps you to remember what you learned.
12. Review Notes Prior To The "Test"
    - This was a no-brainer back at university prior to every test. We all know what cramming is, well, why can't we do it before a session of poker? Reviewing notes only serves to bring back to top of mind what you studied previously.

- Poker Application: If you've been studying cbetting this week, take out your notes prior to your session for a little refresher. Using a one-sheet is especially helpful.

13. One-sheet Notes
    - I know you remember *Cliff's Notes*. Teachers didn't want you to use them and they'd often say, "The test will involve questions NOT found in *Cliff's Notes*." Yeah, sure, like your teacher had the time to read the book, read *Cliff's Notes* and devise new questions not found within. The power of a one sheet is that it condenses all of your studies down to the most important elements.
    - Poker Application: For a week's worth of 3betting studies, you might have as many as 3,000 or more words on what you learned. Distilling that down to the essentials will allow for quick pre-session and in-session reviews. It will also help you to relay the information quickly and simply to your study partners.

14. Asking Questions
    - Not a single class ever went by back in high school or university without students asking questions to clarify and to further instruct on the information presented. We can do the same thing with the poker content we consume and the creators who made it. Further explanation is often needed, especially when trying to learn complicated and complex ideas that can't be transmitted in just a couple sentences.
    - Poker Application: If you listened to one of my podcasts and I said something that confused you or you want to know if the idea is applicable to other areas of poker, just send me an email. I'll always respond.

15. Teaching Poker
    - Einstein said, "If you can't explain it simply, you don't understand it enough." Teaching a topic is the final indication that we know it well enough. Too many poker players never take this step, though. They want to either keep the information to themselves, or they lack confidence in their full understanding of the topic at hand. Plus, teachers learn plenty from their students as well.
    - Poker Application: Every video creator started off by making their first video on a subject they know explicitly. I did, and I

recommend you do the same for yourself. When you planning a video and realize you don't know how to teach it, it's time to hit the books once again.

16. Utilizing a Coach
    - Coaches provide accountability and instruction, helping you get from where you are now to where you want to be. Coaches spot issues in your game that are hidden to you, they don't hold back and tell it like it is and they are a supportive person on your side.
    - Poker Application: Just pull the trigger and hire your first coach. It might take some time to find one that meshes with your style, but they're out there, I guarantee it. You want one that will be honest with you, will help find and fix leaks, will respond to questions quickly out of session, and is reliable. If they don't fit the bill, get the most out of the sessions you paid for then move on.

17. Flash Cards
    - This is one of my favorites. We did this back in school when learning the names of bones in the human body or the state capitals. Rote memorization isn't the best way to get ideas or concepts ingrained in your mind, but it's a start.
    - Poker Application: If you just can't remember how often a ½ pot-sized bluff bet needs to work or a ¾ pot-sized bet, just create flashcards for them and drill yourself over and over until you can recall the information mid-session as you play.
    - I created some flash cards for your use: http://www.smartpokerstudy.com/HTSPflashcards

18. Quizzes
    - Remember the old "Pop Quiz!" back in school? You might not have realized it at the time but they served three important purposes:
    1. To ensure, for the teacher's sake, that you're paying attention
    2. To help you remember what you just learned
    3. The fact that a pop quiz was possible subconsciously stimulated you to pay at least a tiny bit more attention than you would've otherwise
    - Poker Application: With the next bit of content you study and notes you take, create a simple five question pop quiz. Write out the questions and the answers. This could easily be a part

How To Study Poker

of your one sheet, or a separate entity you can review prior to play sessions.

19. Book Reports
    - We started doing these back in elementary school, and I can still remember a few of the books I did them on (my favorite being *James and the Giant Peach*). When you know you have to present to the class or at least write it up so the teacher knows you read the book, you're going to pay a bit more attention, be a bit more critical and analytical, and big events or ideas in the book will be more memorable for you.
    - Poker Application: Do the same with the next poker book you read. Write up a one to two page report (or summary) of all you learned. Get creative and write it as though you were going to publish your review in goodreads.com for others to read.

20. Look After Yourself
    - This is huge (although it's not exactly a study technique). This is more important than any one technique as great health from a proper diet, plenty of exercise and social interaction will go a long way to improving your poker studies and play. Healthy people have more active minds and can push themselves to perform when the going gets tough.
    - Poker Application: Daily meditation, exercise, a green smoothie, plenty of sleep (eight+ hours) and little or no alcohol will make you a poker playing and studying beast. Don't believe me? Try it for a week and see if there's a change in your mood and outlook.

21. Come Prepared
    - Benjamin Franklin said, "By failing to prepare, you are preparing to fail." Preparation isn't always fun (hours and hours of study for example) but it helps you to get the most out of any endeavor and leads to greater success.
    - Poker Application: Before you play in your first main event, great preparation would be lots of LIVE tournament practice, understanding the tournament structure, figuring out when the likely money bubble will break and getting plenty of rest prior to day one. Also, prior to a session with a coach, you'll get more out of the session if you've completed all the work they told you to do, as well as play lots of hands for them to

Utilizing 25 Different (And Simple) Study Techniques

go over and have plenty of questions for them to help you with.

22. Doing The Work
    - It's so easy to get motivated through goal setting and dreaming of "someday..." But doing the work necessary to achieve your dreams is another thing entirely. Poker achievement comes from digging in and studying every aspect of play, actually running the numbers and working out ranges, analyzing opponents and discussing poker with others. Half-assed study by simply watching videos, reading books and forums and listening to podcasts just doesn't cut it.
    - Poker Application: After you create your goals from Part 2, commit yourself to doing the work necessary to achieve them. Is it going to take daily study and play? Then carve out the time and force yourself to do them. Is it going to take more LIVE play in the local cardrooms? Then gas up your car and get your butt over there more often. Once you commit to how you're going to achieve your poker dreams, take action.

23. Game Tape
    - I already covered this in detail back in chapter 17, so I'll just say this here: Game Tape is the most beneficial yet underutilized self-study tool available to you. Use it.
    - Poker Application: Record your session nightly and speak through your thoughts. Review the game tape the next day and record every mistake you and your opponents make. Then commit to not making them again and to exploit them in your opponents.

24. Tick Sheets
    - Tick sheets are great for keeping you focused on one specific task as you play. Every time you complete an action related to the task, you make a tick mark. The goal IS NOT to make a certain number of tick marks, or have some magical ratio of one tick to another. The goal is to keep yourself focused on the task at hand, and making a tick for every focused decision made helps to keep you immersed in the session.
    - Poker Application: If you're working on your "in position" versus "out of position" play, here's what your tick sheet might look like after seeing 14 flops, 8 IP and 6 OOP:

How To Study Poker

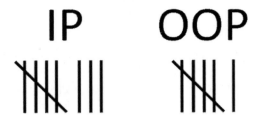

Figure 4: My IP & OOP tick sheet

- You can use tick sheets to help you stay focused on:
    o Value Bets versus Bluff Bets
    o Pre-flop 3bets versus Pre-flop Calls
    o Getting it in ahead versus behind your opponent's hand
    o Your suckouts versus their suckouts
    o And any other session focus you may have

25. Sweat Sessions
    - Sweat sessions take place when you're actually playing poker and a coach or respected poker pal watches over your shoulder. The "sweater" asks the player questions like, "Why did you do that?" or "Are you going for value?" or "What range does your opponent do that with?" or "Why did you use that sizing?" These questions help the player think about the actions that they're making and this is an invaluable tool to help you learn as you play.
    - Poker Application: Set one of these up for yourself and try it out. Your coach would be more than happy.

Action Step #21 – Putting To Use New Techniques

In your next week of study, choose three items from the above list of twenty-five that you've never used before, and put them to use. The more experience you get with all of the study techniques available to you, the better you'll be able to choose the strategies that will offer you the most benefits as your studies progress.

* * * *

— 19 —

Getting The Most From PokerTracker 4: The Best Suite Of Online Tools

"Man is a tool-using animal. Without tools he is nothing, with tools he is all."
-Thomas Carlyle

PokerTracker 4 is the best poker tracking software available, hands down. I've been using it for years and it's at the heart of every one of my study sessions and play sessions.

There are so many built-in features which I love and use frequently:

- An impressive and easy-to-use HUD (heads-up display)
- Many reporting and hand filtering features
- Visually intuitive graphs for viewing results
- Detailed statistics to help you analyze your play and that of your opponents
- Proprietary features like TableTracker, LeakTracker, NoteTracker as well as equity and ICM calculators

How PokerTracker 4 Works

Each poker client you play on, whether it's Americas Cardroom, Pokerstars, 888 or Party Poker, stores the hands you play within a database on your computer's hard drive. This feature enables you to click the little replayer within the software and play back a hand that was just played, or one from an earlier session. This database records every bit of information about the hand: the players, stacks & bet sizes, the exposed hole cards and the board, and all the street by street action.

PokerTracker 4 accesses this database of stored hands and imports the hands into its own database. From that point

How To Study Poker

forward, you have a growing list of hands that you can analyze and learn from. This is what makes PT4 so valuable.

5 Ways That You Can Study & Improve Your Game With PokerTracker 4

1. Utilizing The Statistics Tab

With its enormous database of hands, you can imagine that there's so much we can learn from compiling all those hands and parsing through the information in an organized and calculating way.

But where do we start? I recommend starting with the Statistics Tab.

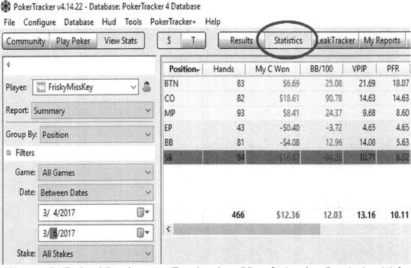

Figure 5: PokerTracker 4 - Reviewing Hands in the Statistics Tab

From the Statistics Tab you can see your game as a whole; how all your hands played add up to the player you are. You can view each important statistic here by position, session, date, stake or even by starting hands.

Once you have the statistics report grouped by one of these factors (position is my preference), you can analyze your statistics. Here are a few examples of insights by position that you could look for to improve your game (there are actually

Getting The Most From PokerTracker 4: The Best Suite Of Online Tools

hundreds of things you could look for, but I will only list a few here to get you started):

Positional Awareness

Are you positionally aware? Strong players use wider ranges as they get to the later positions. They don't play the same 25% of hands from EP and the BTN.

Position	Hands	My C Won	BB/100	VPIP	PFR
BTN	83	$6.69	25.08	21.69	18.07
CO	82	$18.61	90.78	14.63	14.63
MP	93	$8.41	24.37	9.68	8.60
EP	43	-$0.40	-3.72	4.65	4.65
BB	81	-$4.08	12.96	14.08	5.63
SB	84	-$16.87	-84.26	10.71	6.02

Figure 6: PokerTracker 4 – Looking for positional awareness (more hands played in later positions)

Current Win Rate

How does your BB/100 hands win rate flow as you get into the later positions? (Figure 7) Like the number of hands you play, your win rate normally increases as you get to the later positions.

Position	Hands	My C Won	BB/100	VPIP	PFR
BTN	83	$6.69	25.08	21.69	18.07
CO	82	$18.61	90.78	14.63	14.63
MP	93	$8.41	24.37	9.68	8.60
EP	43	-$0.40	-3.72	4.65	4.65
BB	81	-$4.08	12.96	14.08	5.63
SB	84	-$16.87	-84.26	10.71	6.02

Figure 7: PokerTracker 4 – win rates increase as position gets later

Frequency Issues

Frequency issues are areas where your statistics tell your opponents how you approach your hands in specific instances. For example, does your Raise First In percentage jump from the CO to the BTN (Figure 8)? This is indicative of much wider BTN ranges which have a harder time standing up to 3bets from the blinds. Your more observant opponents might notice this and 3bet Resteal more often versus your BTN open raises.

How To Study Poker

Position	Hands	My C Won	BB/100	VPIP	PFR	Call PF 2Bet	Raise First	2Bet PF & Fold
BTN	83	$6.69	25.08	21.69	18.07	8.33	29.55	66.67
CO	82	$18.61	90.78	14.63	14.63	0.00	19.35	0.00
MP	93	$8.41	24.37	9.68	8.60	7.14	10.53	0.00
EP	43	-$0.40	-3.72	4.65	4.65		4.65	100.00
BB	81	-$4.08	12.96	14.08	5.63	10.53		
SB	84	-$16.87	-64.28	10.71	6.02	7.41	25.00	0.00
	466	$12.36	12.03	13.16	10.11	7.91	16.33	42.86

Figure 8: PokerTracker 4 – looking at the jump in Raise First In percentage from the CO to the BTN

Specific Positional Analysis

When you select a specific position, for example CO, the most recent hands played in that position appear below. Now you can sort these hands by amount won, hole cards, pre-flop action or the action you faced, the strength of the winning hand or even the size of the pot in BB's and the rake paid. By seeing all the hands from one position, you can dive into each and find where you're making your biggest mistakes. Sometimes, you may find that two or three big losing hands make up the majority of your losses for one position. While other times, you may find you have a smaller yet consistent leak in a given position.

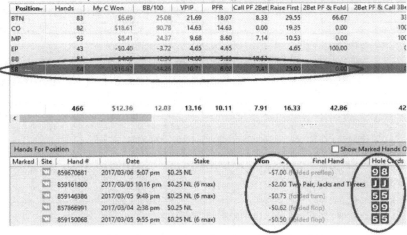

Figure 9: PokerTracker 4 – hands played in the SB, sorted by $Won and viewing the hole cards played

Getting The Most From PokerTracker 4: The Best Suite Of Online Tools

Analyzing Opponents

You can flip the script and view all the hands you have on an opponent as well. Maybe you face a certain winning regular every session named "SAM777." SAM777 multi-tables and has strong statistics. SAM777 is also a beast at the tables who you hate playing against, especially when he has position on you. Using PT4 you can analyze SAM to find specific weaknesses and frequency issues you may be able to exploit. And, you can even incorporate what you learn about SAM777's game to improve your own game.

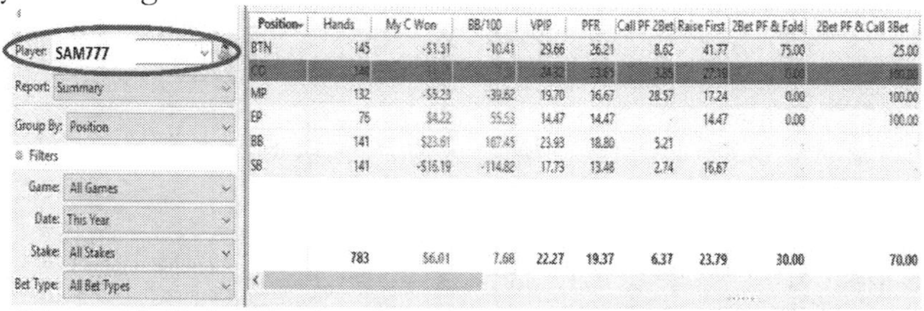

Figure 10: PokerTracker 4 – selecting opponents from the drop down box to analyze their games

2. Filtering Your Database For Specific Situations

Filtering your database for specific scenarios to analyze is one of the best ways to learn from PT4. This is how you drill down and analyze any possible leaks you think you may have.

Example. Your cbet frequency drops from 70% on the flop to 35% on the turn. The best way to analyze this situation is to filter for all hands where you had the opportunity to cbet the turn but didn't. Within the filter "Actions and Opportunities" filter, select "Bet Flop Continuation Bet" and "Checked Turn".

How To Study Poker

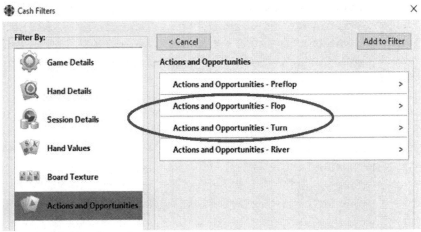

Figure 11: Finding the "Actions and Opportunities" Tab with the Flop & Turn options

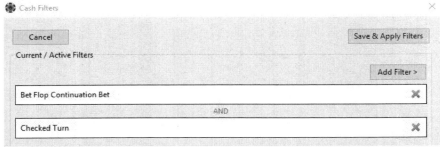

Figure 12: Cbet Flop and Checked Turn filters display

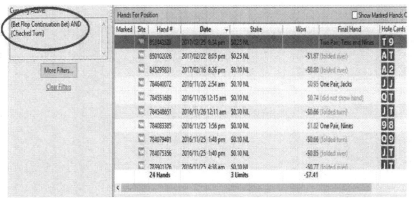

Figure 13: The results from the Cbet Flop and Checked Turn filter

Bam! Every hand now displayed shows you cbetting the flop then following that up with a turn check. You can dive into each of these and determine whether a turn cbet was in order and if you made a mistake by not cbetting. Also, you can determine if that first flop cbet was itself a profitable play.

You can also filter for when you actually made the turn cbet to see the profitability of firing that double barrel.

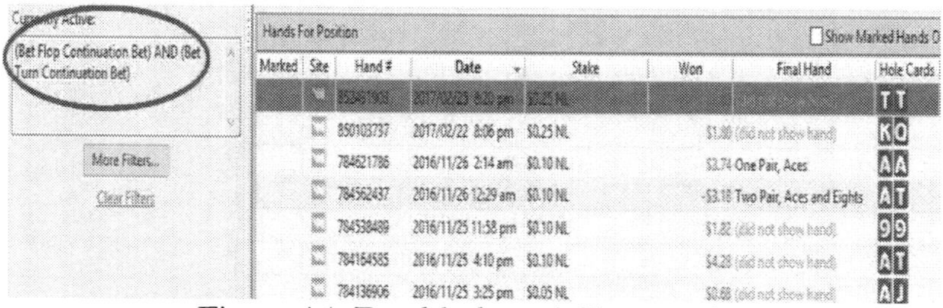

Figure 14: Double-barrel filter results

There are so many ways to utilize the filters within PT4 to analyze your game. You've to get in there and get your hands and brain dirty testing it. To get you started, here are five of my favorite leak finding and game improving filters:

1. How profitable are you when calling turn raises?

2. How profitable are you when calling 3bets OOP (out of position)?

3. What about calling 3bets IP (in position)?

4. Are you a winning player when you're calling the flop and turn (being passive)?

5. What about when you're betting the flop and the turn (being aggressive)?

3. Utilizing A Heads-up Display (HUD)

Most of us use PokerTracker 4 in the first place for the HUD. It gives us real-time statistics on our opponents that accumulate as we play with them.

How To Study Poker

You can configure it any way you like with hundreds of different statistics, but the most common statistics to see are (definitions for these begin in chapter 20 where I'll dive deeply into HUD statistics):

- VPIP and PFR
- 3bet and Fold to 3bet
- Cbet and Fold to Cbet
- Attempt to Steal or Fold to Steal

Figure 15: Cash Game Smart HUD on the virtual felt

The HUD gets more useful as we play more with an opponent. Over just 10 hands it does not tell you much. But as we get 50, then 100, 200, 500 and ultimately 1,000's of hands on opponents, the statistics we get from those hands can lead us to their weaknesses and ways to exploit them.

Example: Imagine your database contains 500 hands on each of two opponents. One folds to steals 85% of the time, and the other 50%. Which will you steal more against? I'm sure you're correct; the one who folds 85% of the time.

These two same players, one has a River AFq of just 25%, the other has an AFq of 45% (AFq is the percentage of non-checking action taken on any one street, and it's a measurement of how aggressive they are). Against which player can you call more often on the river with top pair, weak kicker? You guessed it, the guy that has an AFq of 45%. The more aggressive, the more likely they bet with less than top pair.

Another great benefit of utilizing the HUD for in-game play is the hand tagging feature. As you play, you'll come across many hands that either confuse you or make you want to dive in and study the situation. Tag these hands for your next review session.

Getting The Most From PokerTracker 4: The Best Suite Of Online Tools

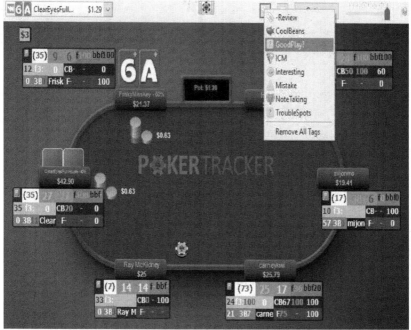

Figure 16: Tagging a hand with "GoodPlay?"

4. Finding Cash Game Leaks With LeakTracker

PokerTracker 4 has a great feature called LeakTracker for cash games.

When you run the LeakTracker feature, it analyzes your database and shows you how your statistics compare to those of winning players at 6max and full-ring games.

How To Study Poker

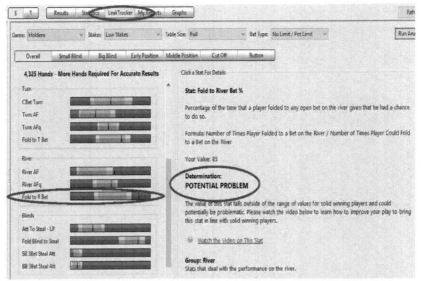

Figure 17: LeakTracker showing me I have a potential problem with folding too frequently on the river

Of course, there's no perfect number for any statistic as each exists along a spectrum. One cannot say that the best players only play 20% of hands. Sure, across all positions it's 20%, but it's less in the EP's and more in the later positions.

With each statistic presented, say for example SB 3bet versus Steal Attempt, it shows you if you're high or low, gives info on the statistic in case you don't understand it, and there's a linked video to watch which explains the statistic in greater detail.

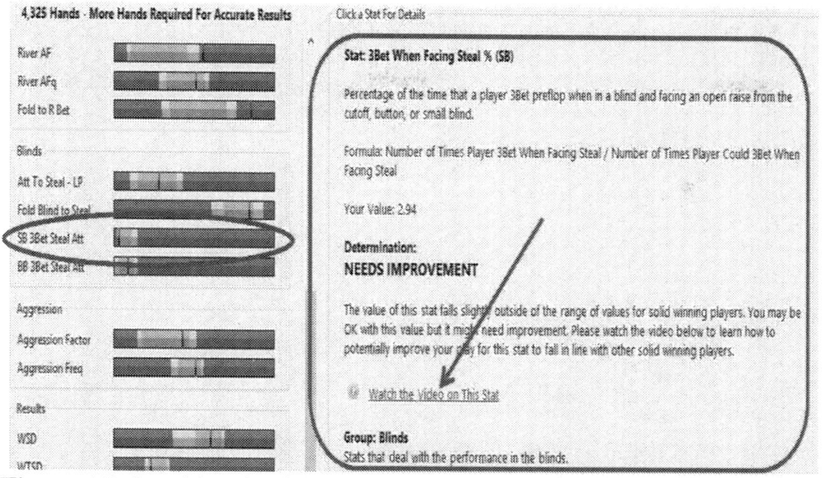

Getting The Most From PokerTracker 4: The Best Suite Of Online Tools

Figure 18: Looking in detail at the "SB 3bet Steal Att" statistic and related information with training video available

Now that you know what areas you have possible leaks in, you can return to the filtering feature of PT4 and filter for hands relevant to your leak. Following the SB 3bet versus Steal Attempt example (which is one of my leaks), I can filter for situations where I faced an open raise while in the SB but chose not to 3bet with hands I determine are 3bet worthy for value or as bluffs. (Figure 19 for filters, Figure 20 for results).

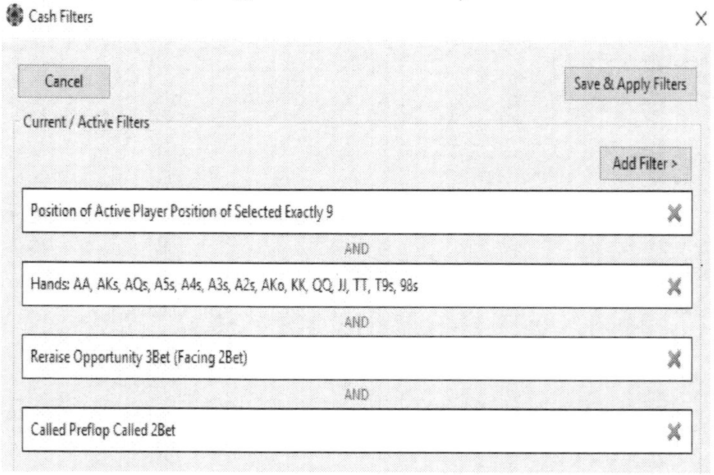

Figure 19: The filter parameters for SB hands where I failed to 3bet and called instead

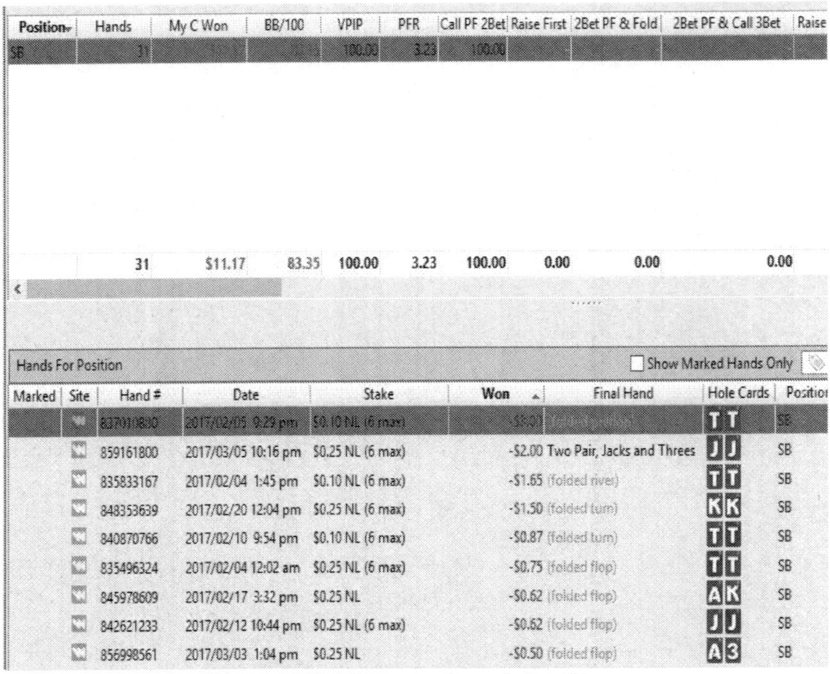

How To Study Poker

Figure 20: The results of the filter

After running this filter I can review the resulting hands and determine if I made a correct decision by not 3betting. This kind of review will help me when I encounter this very frequent situation in the future.

Even if you're an MTT or SNG player, many of these cash game LeakTracker videos will help you out. They give great insights into many individual statistics, and understanding how they work for cash games can aid your MTT and SNG use of them.

5. Sharing Hands

One great way to study is to share these perfectly recorded hands with friends, forums or your coach to get feedback on your play.

Getting The Most From PokerTracker 4: The Best Suite Of Online Tools

Figure 21: Posting one of my own hands from PT4 in the Smart Poker Study Podcast FB Group

These hands contain the unvarnished truth because they show exactly what happened. You want honest feedback on your game, and showing your advisors what mistakes you may have made can lead to great improvements. Often the players who comment on hands will notice things you never did: "Did you see how aggressive that BTN was? Did you consider that before you made the third overlimp pre-flop?"

Two heads are better than one when it comes to reviewing hands, and 15 heads even better yet! So post some hands in forums or even better yet, post them in the **SPS Facebook Group** at http://www.smartpokerstudy.com/discuss.

Action Step #22 – Utilize PokerTracker 4

If you're not using it already, start a free trial of PokerTracker 4 to improve your game today. Visit my affiliate link to download the software and start your free 30 day trial: http://www.smartpokerstudy.com/pokertracker4

Once you have the program (or if you already use it), then get more out of the software. Commit to using the software for an hour a day over the next five days.

Day 1: Review your entire current month of play, starting with your statistics and look at them by position. What positions are you an inordinate loser (BB/100) or where are you playing way too many hands? Dive into the related hands and try to determine what the problem is.

Day 2: Test the filters and start by filtering for opportunities to cbet and review those hands. Are you making cbetting mistakes?

Day 3: Improve your HUD by adding/subtracting statistics as you feel is necessary to improve your in-game reads.

Day 4: Use LeakTracker and see what it tells you about your cash game leaks. Head back to the filters to analyze the areas that LeakTracker alerts you to.

Day 5: Drop a couple hand histories in the Smart Poker Study FB Discussion Group and ask for some opinions on your play.

* * * *

Once you dive into PokerTracker 4 and start using it, new ideas will occur to you and the additional features like NoteTracker and TableTracker will be of much use as well.

Most aspects of PT4 study revolve around the various statistics we use to analyze our game and that of our opponents. In the next chapter I will cover the most useful statistics, what each of them mean and what information you can glean from them.

— 20 —
PokerTracker 4: Common Statistics For Analysis

"Analysis is the critical starting point of strategic thinking."
-Kenichi Ohmae

PokerTracker 4 comes with roughly 400 statistics to help you analyze your game and that of your opponents.

You can find the complete list of statistics with descriptions and the formula for the calculation of each within the 'Configure' submenu at the top of the screen.

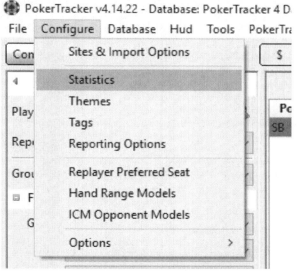

Figure 22: Where to find information on PT4's Statistics

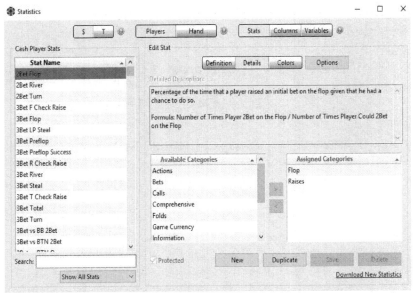

Figure 23: The Statistics selection screen with description and formula

    Below, I share my list of most useful statistics as a quick reference for you. With the description and formula for each, I include five bullet points of the most important information you need to assess each statistic.

    Every statistic listed here is contained within my custom SMART HUD and Popups. This allows me to keep all the relevant decision making details at my fingertips while I play. PokerTracker allows you to customize the HUD, and you can tailor it to your needs like I did. For an idea of how robust and useful a HUD can be, checkout screen shots of my SMART HUD and Popups by going to http://www.smartpokerstudy.com/SmartHUD.

VPIP–Voluntarily Put $ in the Pot

Description: Percentage of the time that a player voluntarily contributed money to the pot, given that he had a chance to do so. The key is "voluntarily."

Formula: Number of Times Player Put Money In Pot / (Number of Hands - Number of Walks)

- This statistic becomes useful starting with the first hand played. Very reliable at 50+ hands.
- This is the most powerful statistic there is as it's calculated in every hand played and is a great indication of how active a player is and what range of hands they play.
- The higher the percentage, the more hands played, the fishier the player. 30% means they play 30% of the hands dealt to them.
- If you're not playing enough hands, you become predictably nitty; while playing too many hands gives you weak ranges on each street relative to your opponent's range.
- To decrease your VPIP, play less OOP and do not limp any hands. Call less from the blinds as well. Playing tighter ranges also simplifies post-flop play.
- To increase your VPIP, play more often IP and add suited connectors, decent suited A's and K's and small pocket pairs.
- To learn the VPIP percentages of the average winning player (and the other statistics listed here), you can go to https://www.pokertracker.com/videos/PT4/leaktracker to watch the PokerTracker 4 LeakTracker training video related to each statistic.

PFR–Pre-flop Raise

Description: Percentage of the time that a player puts in any raise pre-flop, given that he had a chance to do so.
Formula: Number of Times Player Raised Pre-flop / (Number of Hands - Number of Walks)

- This statistic becomes useful starting with the first hand played. Very reliable at 50+ hands.
- This is counted every time you make any type of raise (2b/3b+) and indicates aggression (high = wants to build pots, low = passivity).
- This is a great indicator of their raising range, so use the percentage to estimate the range of hands they play using Flopzilla or another hand range visualizer.
- To increase your PFR%, open wider IP, avoid playing hands OOP and don't limp.
  - Pre-flop aggression tends to carry over to post-flop play.

- PFR is very useful on its own, but gains greater significance when coupled with VPIP.

Gap Between VPIP & PFR

Description: The difference between these two percentages is how often they call or limp pre-flop instead of raising. It's a measure of passivity. The bigger the gap, the more they call or limp pre-flop.

Formula: PT4 doesn't calculate this, it's simply the VPIP percentage minus the PFR percentage.

- This gap becomes useful starting with the first hand played. Very reliable at 50+ hands.
- These are the most important statistics to look at when making pre-flop decisions. You need enough pre-flop aggression in poker to take advantage of the timidity of other players and to have initiative post-flop.
- Combining VPIP with PFR tells you how passive or aggressive an opponent is.
    o Example: 12/9 (VPIP/PFR) player – Nitty yet aggressive – this player only plays 12% of hands overall, and raises 9% of those hands, just calling with the other 3%. So they raise 75% of the hands they play and call the other 25% of hands.
    o Example: 30/10 player – Loose yet passive – plays a wide 30% of hands, but only comes in for a raise 33% of the time.
- You need to be raising <u>at least ½ of the hands you play</u>, preferably at 75%+. If you're raising less, you just aren't being aggressive enough pre-flop and you're relying on hitting hands on the flop to win you pots.
- The bigger the gap between VPIP & PFR, the more often they cold-call bets or limp in. Narrow gaps are more aggressive.
- Most fish have a large gap which means they are passive players and they have a passive and weak pre-flop strategy as they call too often. Aggressive players have a small gap and come in for lots of raises to steal pots pre-flop.

3bet Pre-flop

Description: Percentage of the time that a player 3Bet pre-flop given that he had a chance to do so.
Formula: Number of 3Bets Pre-flop / Number of Times Player Could 3Bet Pre-flop

- This statistic becomes useful starting at 100+ hands, very reliable at 500+ hands.
- This is the most commonly viewed statistic to see how aggressive an opponent is.
- Low 3bet suggests the player only re-raises with very strong hands (like 2-3% being only QQ+ and AK). We can raise their blinds often knowing they'll only come back over the top with premium hands, and we can expect them to call or fold more often if they have position on us after we 2bet pre-flop.
- High 3bet indicates a greater chance we will face a reraise. If we're raising or opening light (weak) we need to recognize this and be prepared to either fold, 4bet bluff or call with the plan of taking the pot away on a later street.
- When considering making a 3bet always know what you will do if you face more aggression. When bluffing, look for a high Fold to 3bet stat on your opponent.
- When calling a 3bet always have a post-flop plan and know how you will go for value or bluff them off their hand.

ATS–Attempt to Steal

Description: Percentage of the time that a player opened the pot by raising from the cutoff, button, or small blind.
Formula: Number of Times Player Attempted to Steal Blinds / Number of Times Player Could Attempt to Steal Blinds

- This statistic becomes useful starting at 50+ hands, very reliable at 200+ hands.
- You need to steal the blinds/antes from tight blinds every chance you get, whether in tourneys or cash games.
- Versus high ATS players, consider coming over the top with a 3bet Steal from the blinds. View their Fold to 3bet statistic first and look for a high percentage.

- Your BB win rate in 'Chance to Steal' situations ought to be at least double that of your overall BB win rate as you need to take advantage of this every time the opportunity presents itself.
- By increasing your steal%, you also increase the chances that you're playing a hand IP, which translates to more $ won by having the advantage of acting after your opponents more often.
- Before you attempt to steal, check your opponent's statistics:
  o VPIP and PFR looking nitty or passive (12/8 or 25/10).
  o Check their 3bet % and if high, reconsider stealing with the bottom of your range and only do so with hands you'll 4bet with or open/call.
  o Check their post flop statistics, namely Fold to Flop/Turn Cbet, Flop Donk bet and Flop Float bet to gauge how likely you're to face post-flop aggression.

Cbet Flop–Continuation Bet Flop

Description: Percentage of the time that a player bets the flop given that he had a chance to do so and he made the last raise pre-flop.

Formula: Number of Times Player Continuation Bet on the Flop / Number of Times Player Could Continuation Bet on the Flop

- This statistic becomes useful starting at 100+ hands, very reliable at 500+ hands.
- Your Cbet% needs to be 50%+ or else you're too passive <u>with initiative</u> post flop. Initiative and aggression win most pots post-flop, so continuing for value and with bluffs are both profitable plays, especially when IP and versus weak players.
- Your default play is to cbet. But don't cbet when doing so seems to be a losing situation (out of position on a flop with no equity; flop hits opponent's range way more than yours; opponent calls every flop cbet and you don't have the equity/outs to double-barrel; the opponent check-raises or raises cbets a lot and you can't defend against this with your range on this board).

- Most ranges only hit TP+ and decent draws 35% of the time. If you only cbet when you hit, then you will be highly predictable. Similarly, look for opponents who only cbet 35% of the time. If you encounter such a low cbet from a pre-flop raiser, you can blow them off most checked flops.
- In general, tight players are fit or fold post-flop and must be cbet bluffed frequently. Overly passive players love to call down, so bluff them less but go for extra value when you have a hand stronger than what they can likely call you with.
- If you're facing a cbet from an active cbettor (65%+ Cbet), this is often just a bluff so consider a check-raise, cbet raise, or a float with intent on taking it away on the turn.

Combo Statistic: Flop Cbet & Turn Cbet

- These statistics becomes useful together starting at 100+ hands, very reliable at 500+ hands.
- These two statistics together show you which street a player gets honest on.
    - Flop Cbet at 70% and Turn at 30% means they are "turn honest" and only bet the turn with a strong hand
    - Flop Cbet at 80% and Turn at 70% means they are not honest at all on the flop or turn and are constant double-barrel bluffers
- Whichever street he gets 'honest' on is where you'll decide whether or not to make your bluff play based on any opening he may give you. If you're facing an opponent who does not appear to double-barrel bluff (they have a high Flop Cbet and low Turn Cbet) you can check-call or call IP on the flop and plan to fold to his 'honest' turn bet. If you're in position, you will take the pot away with a bet once they check the turn to you.

Action Step #23 – Learn Statistics For Yourself

The list just presented is only a start to your statistics learning. Find the following statistics within PokerTracker 4 for yourself. Learn the descriptions and the formulas, then bullet point 3 different important aspects of each for yourself.

Fold to Flop Cbet
Description:

Formula:

-

-

-

Fold to Pre-flop 3bet
Description:

Formula:

-

-

-

* * * *

Here's a killer PDF I created for you: The Top 10 Poker HUD Stats. It contains names and descriptions of the most important statistics, as well as ways to exploit frequency issues that these statistics highlight in your opponent's games. It also provides you with statistical ranges for your average winning players. Download it now: http://www.smartpokerstudy.com/HTSPtop10hudstats.

PokerTracker 4 is an incredible software package, but it can't do everything for you. The other piece of essential software I recommend is Flopzilla. If you do not have experience with this incredible program yet, get ready to be blown away.

— 21 —

Getting The Most From Flopzilla: The Best Calculating Software

"Give ordinary people the right tools, and they will design and build the most extraordinary things."
-Neil Gershenfeld

Flopzilla is an amazing program and has been instrumental in my understanding of ranges and the interactions between ranges and various boards. This is the sole purpose of Flopzilla: figuring out how a range hits the board.

I'm going to keep the text here pretty short and sweet because reading about Flopzilla will not help you much; seeing it in action, and then using it for yourself is where the benefit lies. At the end of this chapter, after I espouse some features of Flopzilla with details and screenshots, I will list some of the best Flopzilla instructional videos found on YouTube.

Benefit: Improved Range Visualization

Consistent use of Flopzilla has helped me to better visualize ranges. The reason for this is simple; all of your work in Flopzilla deals with inputting and changing ranges for varying situations and opponents.

Due to all this practice, I can conjure in my mind what a 5% or 15% or 30% range looks like (Figure 24). With the ability to visualize ranges, I have a better idea of what my opponents are likely playing given their pre-flop actions, and I can keep this range in my thoughts longer as the hand progresses.

How To Study Poker

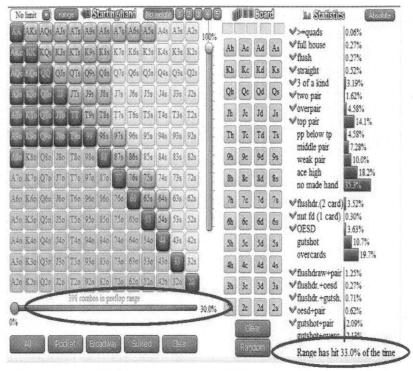

Figure 24: A 30% opening range (398 combos) in Flopzilla that "hits" the flop 33% of the time

Constant work with Flopzilla increases your understanding of "percentage form" as well. This key skill for online players who use HUDs relates info to you in percentage-form, but it also helps LIVE players. If you estimate a player opens the BTN 30% of the time, or your HUD statistics tell you as much, you know he is likely opening any pocket pair, A5s and A8o or better, every suited 8+ and every off-suit 9+, and 54s+ and 64s+.

Benefit: Understanding Range & Board Interaction

Until I used Flopzilla I had no idea how to calculate how often a range of hands hit a board. How often does the 30% range above hit a JT7r board? "Hitting the board" means TP+, an oesd or pair+draw. The answer is 50%.

Getting The Most From Flopzilla: The Best Calculating Software

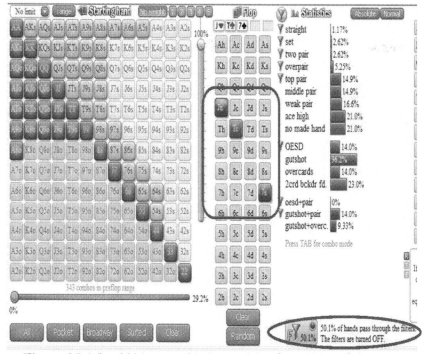

Figure 25: The 30% range hitting a JT7r flop 50% of the time

The reason this hits so frequently is because the 30% range consists of lots of broadway and middle cards which hits this type of board well. Practice like this has helped me to see the type of boards that different ranges hit strongly, which helps me avoid costly flop cbets or check-raises or donk bets that will fail to elicit the fold I'm looking for.

Benefit: Seeing Future Cards & Effects On Equity

Another great aspect of Flopzilla is seeing how different flops affect equities, and what future cards can do to it. If we look at that same 30% range versus the hand of AA on the JT7r flop, we see the AA has 74% equity* (Figure 26). That equity drops to 69% on a turn Qd (Figure 27). But the AA equity increases to 81% on a turn 3d (Figure 28).

*Equity is how often a given hand or range can expect to win versus another hand or range at that moment once all the

How To Study Poker

cards are dealt. Equity changes on a street by street basis as new board cards are dealt.

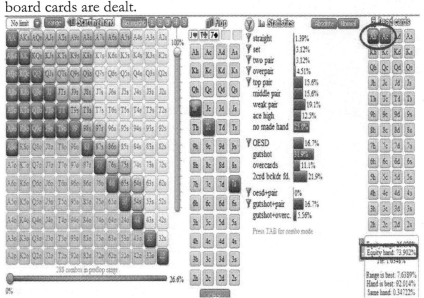

Figure 26: AA has 74% equity vs the 30% range on JT7r

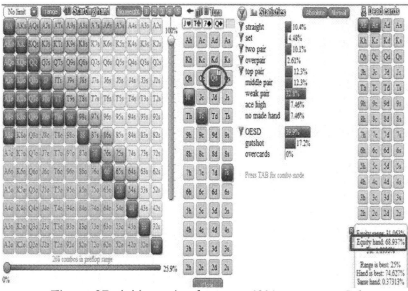

Figure 27: AA's equity drops to 69% on a turn Qd

Getting The Most From Flopzilla: The Best Calculating Software

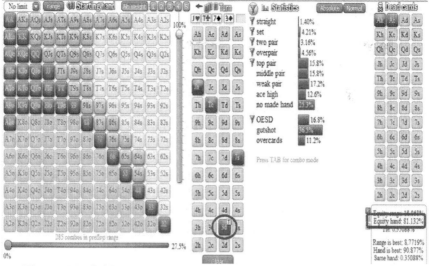

Figure 28: AA's equity increases greatly to 81% on a turn 3d

Working with Flopzilla this way gets you to start thinking about the effects of future cards, which translates to your in-game play. This helps you develop plans for future cards while at the tables and involved in a hand. If you know what helps your range and hurts your opponent's on the next street, or vice versa, you can make plans for the cards that come.

Benefit: Improved Combo Counting

Not only does Flopzilla display ranges in percentage form, but can also display ranges and statistics in card combo form. For example, that prior 30% range consists of 288 combos once we remove the board cards and our AA. This range "hits" the flop 56% of the time with 161 hands (161/288). For many poker players, these hard numbers seem easier to understand than percentage form.

How To Study Poker

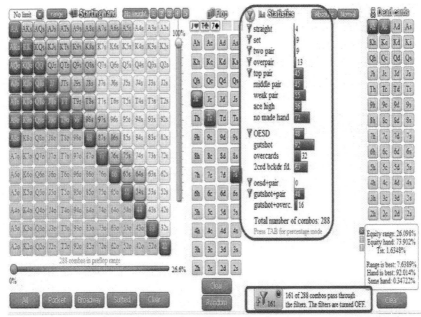

Figure 29: Looking at combos instead of percentages within the Statistics section

Looking at analyses in combo form helps us spot huge frequency issues in our game.

Example: Say we get to the flop with a player, we cbet 90 combos of hands we have, but if he check-shoves for a pot-sized bet, we would only call with our 9 combos of sets. Well, this means we're only calling 9 out of 90 combos or only 10% of the time. His check-shove only needs to work 50%, but it's working 90% of the time.

He is printing money by shoving 100% of the time versus us in this spot, and we're incredibly exploitable due to our folding 90% of the time. Finding and correcting these frequency issues can plug many holes in our game.

Benefit: Narrowing Ranges As The Hand Progresses

The statistics section allows you to narrow the range as you progress in the hand. Within the statistics section it will show you the percentage of the range that hits a specific hand, whether it's a

TP, set, fd, no made hand, whatever. You can begin to narrow the range by filtering for these specific hands.

With the 30% range (288 combos) on JT7r example, with us holding AA, let's say our opponent only continues beyond the flop with TP+, an open-ended straight draw (oesd) or pair + draw.

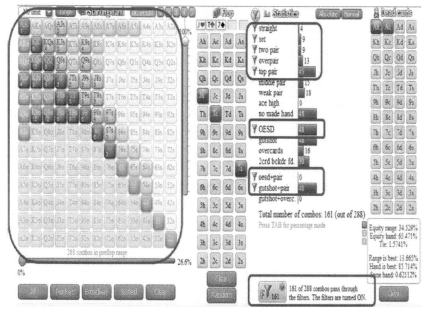

Figure 30: Our opponent's range narrows from 288 combos to 161 (the grey hands were dropped out) if we think they only continue with TP+, oesd's and pair+draws

From Figure 30, we see he only continues with 161 combos of his original range, and it shows which hands still remain that fit the criteria we set. The software removes hands from his range that do not meet the criteria. I'm sure you can see how valuable this aspect of Flopzilla is to hand reading. You don't have to mark hands off on a piece of paper or painstakingly consider each one in Pokerstove and manually remove them from the matrix.

Great Flopzilla Instructional Videos On YouTube

Splitsuit: 'How To Use Flopzilla' – this is the perfect video to begin your Flopzilla education. Just search "Splitsuit Flopzilla" within YouTube to find this video.

Smart Poker Study: 'Using Flopzilla to Range Opponents' – in this video I use Flopzilla to range our opponent from start to finish and determine whether to call or fold w/ AKs on a monotone K87 flop. Visit www.youtube.com/smartpokerstudy to find my video channel.

Smart Poker Study: 'Using Flopzilla and HoldEq to do Range v Range Equity Analysis'– I demonstrate how to use Flopzilla and HoldEq together for range versus range equity calculations. I also show how to look at the post-flop playability of a range, and how to compare an opening range to a cold calling range.

Action Step #24 – Get Into Flopzilla

If you don't have Flopzilla yet, purchase it NOW as it's only $35 and is the best money you will spend in poker.
www.flopzilla.com

Watch the three videos listed above to begin your training.

Next, get familiar with Flopzilla by doing some hand reading practice with showdown hands from your database. See how accurate you are in your final assessment of the opponent's range.

* * * *

With the introduction to PokerTracker 4 and Flopzilla complete, let's see how I use these two programs in conjunction the most: hand history reviews.

— 22 —

Hand History Reviews For Analyzing Your Game And Finding Leaks

"The more you know about the past, the better prepared you are for the future."
-Theodore Roosevelt

To improve as a poker player, you need to go beyond reading books and watching videos. You must review your hands to learn about your play, to find your leaks and to analyze the profitability of your decisions.

As discussed, PT4 saves all of your hands and the details of each. The nifty built-in hand replayer allows you to watch the action unfold (instead of just reading the text version hand history you see posted in forums). Watching your hands replay this way allows you to go back and forth in time, to observe the actions, bet sizings, board cards and player statistics at the time of the hand. All this information is critical in analyzing the hand.

My hand history reviews all follow a general four step path, no matter what type of hands I am reviewing.

Questions

Throughout the four steps below, I'm asking myself different questions to help me think about the action. This is by no means a complete list, various situations require different questions to dissect the action. Use this list as ideas for questions you can ask of yourself.

- Is this a minus or plus EV situation for me?
- What would the opponent do with a flush/straight draw, made hand, A high?

How To Study Poker

- How can I <u>bluff/get more value</u>?
- What part of their range will <u>fold/call/raise</u> here?
- What does the opponent's <u>3bet/PFR/Cbet percentage</u> mean for their range?
- What's the opponent hoping for with that play?
- What does the opponent think about my hand on the <u>flop/turn/river</u>?
- How many combos of <u>TP/underpair/flush draws</u> does the opponent have?
- How many combos can they <u>call/raise/3bet</u> here?

1. Choose Hands For Review

You generally don't just go in and choose random hands to review. Make sure you review more than solely your biggest winning/losing hands from the prior session. Get more granular and filter or search through your database for key things you want to work on.

Some examples:

- Pre-flop 3bet hands
- How you approach "tough" hands like TT, JJ and AQ
- Hands where you Cbet/folded on the flop
- Flopped flush or straight draws
- Double-barrel opportunities
- Showdown hands where you bet or called the river
- Non-showdown hands where you folded to a river bet
  Of course, you can also review the hands you tagged during your play sessions with the HUD's hand tagging feature which I discussed back in chapter 19.

2. Begin By Assigning Ranges And Viewing Equities

Every hand worth reviewing will give you the opportunity to whip out Flopzilla and assign your opponent a range of hands. Enter your hand as well to view its equity versus the range you assigned.

Do things like count combos, see how often the range hits the flop, and get a general feel for the situation at hand.

Don't forget to ask yourself questions (like the ones above) to help you think critically about your opponent's range (and your own perceived range).

3. Narrow The Range In Light Of Actions Taken

As the hand progresses, you can narrow the opponent's range based on the actions taken. I'm sure you watched the Smart Poker Study video called 'Using Flopzilla to Range Opponents' that I mentioned in the previous chapter. Use that video as a guide in how to range opponents for yourself within Flopzilla.

Ask questions to help you think critically as you progress through the streets.

PRO TIP: I produced an entire series of podcast based on hand reading and I suggest you listen to the 10-episode series starting with podcast #64.

4. Use Flopzilla To Test Variables

By doing all your work in Flopzilla you can easily change the variables of the hand to see how different ranges, board cards and actions might affect things.

- Change the range you originally assigned your opponent
- Change the board cards (flop, turn or river) to see how different cards interact with the assigned range
- Choose different actions for your opponent, like check-calling instead of donk leading, and see how that changes their range
As you change variables, constantly ask questions (like those mentioned above) to help you think critically.

Action Step #25 – Five Days Of 5x Hand History Reviews

Give yourself lots of practice over the next 5 days by reviewing 5 hands per day. Review the hands and learn what you can about your play and that of your opponents.

How To Study Poker

Each day, choose five hands from your database to do a review on. Here is a list of topics I recommend (5x5 = 25 total hands reviewed):

Day 1: 5x pre-flop 3bet hands

Day 2: 5x "tough" hands like TT, JJ and AQ

Day 3: 5x hands where you Cbet/folded on the flop

Day 4: 5x flopped flush or straight draws

Day 5: 5x showdown hands where you called the river

* * * *

— 23 —

Learning From Poker Strategy Content

The capacity to learn is a gift; The ability to learn is a skill; The willingness to learn is a choice."
-Brian Herbert

When it comes to off-the-felt work, too many poker players just passively consume poker strategy content. We have all been guilty of more than one of these in the past:

- Books: Reading in a matter of days and not putting to use a single idea from the book
- Videos: Watching without taking notes
- Podcasts: Giving them half our attention as we go about running errands or doing chores
- Study Groups: Not contributing fully and letting others do the work while we sit there and nod our heads
- Articles: Quickly scanning through and forgetting it five minutes later as we surf the web
- Forums: Responding to posts with one sentence answers to questions and posted hand histories, and we accept those same worthless responses when we post a hand of our own (if we ever even do that)
- Coaching: Failing to do the homework prior to a session; nor do we even bring any specific questions or scenarios to our coach
- Online Courses: Failing to complete a course we purchased for $197

We often treat simply viewing/reading/listening/suffering through the strategy content as the end goal, as THE THING that will complete our studies on a topic before moving on to the next.

PRO TIP: Take at least one action step away from every piece of poker content you consume. Make that your focus in your next play session. Drill it, practice it, look for spots where you can use what you learned.

Consuming any one piece of poker strategy content must not be the end goal. The content you consume must supplement the other work you do off the felt.

Example: If your theme of study for this week is 3betting, then your effort is best utilized within hand history reviews, filtering through your database, working out ranges with Flopzilla, adding statistics to your HUD/popups, and gaining a greater understanding and appreciation for those 3bet related statistics.

Use poker strategy content as food for thought as you work out strategies for yourself. When you hear Alex Fitzgerald say, "bluff 3bet hands are best when just outside of your calling range," you must do more than just accept it. This is your opportunity to take his statement and put it to the test. Look at your calling 2bet range in a given position. Maybe the worst King you would call is KTs and the worst Queen is QTs. Is it actually effective to 3bet bluff with K9s and Q9s? Are these hands more profitable to 3bet over suited Aces and mid-suited connectors? If you put K9s and Q9s in your 3bet bluff range, what hands do you have to remove to stay balanced?

The goal with this chapter is to get you to approach using poker strategy content as a supplement within the poker study plan you created back in chapter 10. I also want you to approach it more actively. The rewards of active participation far exceed those of passive learning. (We all know that learning is best accomplished by doing.)

For the rest of this chapter, I will use study strategies discussed back in chapter 18 that you can employ with each form of poker content to be a more active consumer. Once I discuss a strategy to use in one form (like Questions & Requests under Videos or Note Taking under Podcasts below), I will not mention it within another. But the strategies apply to more than one form, so pick what works for you and go to town on that perfect piece of poker content you picked-up.

Learning From Books With My '7 Steps To Poker Book Learning PDF'

Any poker strategy book is best consumed in pieces over a long stretch of time. When I read 'The Course' by Ed Miller for the first time, I spent ten weeks reading it by spending a full week on each "Skill." (This book covers ten skills to master for LIVE cash games.) By spending a full week on each skill, I thoroughly studied each and integrated them into my game.

Now, I could list all seven steps I use when studying poker books, but I'm positive that you already downloaded the pdf when I mentioned it in Action Step #1. That is the best way I know of to get the most from the poker books you read. Just in case you haven't already downloaded the pdf, do it now.

Learning From Videos With Questions And Requests

As content producers, coaches like me love to receive questions about what we're teaching. It shows that you're motivated to learn and that our lessons are not falling on deaf ears. And it motivates us to keep on keepin' on. When we know people get something out of what we teach, it fuels us to teach even more.

Show us you care by sending us questions that help you to better understand the content we provided. Sometimes we say things that we fail to fully backup with examples or proof, or we discuss something that brings up a related topic to mind that you think we can help with.

You can contact your favorite content creators in many ways:
- E-mail
- Forum questions
- Twitter, Skype and other social media

And, don't hesitate to send in requests. A subscriber to my YouTube channel watched one of my PokerTracker 4 videos, then requested within the comments for another video on creating a pop-up within PT4. You know what I did? I obliged and within a week recorded and posted another video just for him. Now, others will get something out of it, but he got specifically what he was looking for, and for free. So send in your requests to all your favorite poker strategy creators, because the worst thing they can do is ignore the request.

Some quotes to spur you into action and begin asking questions:

"Knowledge is having the right answer. Intelligence is asking the right question."
-unknown

"He who is afraid to ask is ashamed of learning."
-Danish Proverb

Learning From Podcasts By Taking Notes

Podcasts can be tough to learn from because many of us listen to them passively while doing other things. This is the least active form of study. So, we need to do something to make it active.

When I started listening to the OneOuter Podcast with Alex Fitzgerald and Barry Chalmers, I was enamored with the awesome content Alex was giving away free. The problem was that he answered questions off the cuff with his many years of experience, and there were no show notes to fall back on to help me follow along.

So, what I was forced to do (more accurately, what I made myself do) was to take copious notes on each topic elucidated on. By the end of seventy-five episodes, I had a 10,000 word document full of strategy insights that Alex quickly and easily rattled off responding to questions asked.

Know what else I did? As mentioned under 'Books' above, I asked questions and Alex and Barry responded on the podcast. I learned from the questions of others, as well as my own questions. This benefited my MTT game immensely and I became a better player for the notes I took, the questions I asked, and using the newly learned skills.

And another quick benefit, I sent Alex my notes. He was super appreciative of this as he didn't keep track of all the things he said on the podcast. As a thank-you, he gave me my choice of any of his extremely valuable webinars. What a great guy.

Learning From Study Groups By Taking A Leadership Role

Study groups are great for learning when there is a person dedicated to organizing it, selecting topics to study, holding people accountable for showing up and participating, and keeping the study sessions on track. Most groups fall apart without a "Dungeon Master" at the helm.

So to solve this problem and to help everyone get as much as possible from the group, you can choose to be the "leader" of your group whether in name or through your actions.

Be the organizer. Set dates and times for study sessions. E-mail the participants ahead and remind them of the time and the topic of study. Hold them accountable for not showing up by contacting them later and telling them you missed their insights into _____ topic.

Create topics of study and come to each session fully prepared to teach the subject matter. Be careful, though. Don't act like the teacher. This is a study group session, not a coaching session. You want to express all of your opinions and ideas, but you're not giving a lecture or coaching them. Start with one point at a time and elicit feedback and thoughts from others.

Example: If you're leading a study session all about double-barreling, come prepared with 2 or 3 hands to discuss. You must have your thoughts put together and listed out so you can hit every point. Know these hands inside and out, run the math and do the Flopzilla work ahead of time. Come prepared with your own questions as well.

Keep the study session flowing. If the train starts to go off the rails, gently guide it back on track. Take note of poker-related tangents, and get back to them later or make it a separate topic of discussion for a later session.

At every study session, you must be the most prepared of the participants just as if you were the teacher. I will discuss this in the next chapter, but if you prepare with the idea of having to teach the subject matter in mind, you will learn the subject matter better than if you were just studying for your own sake.

Learning From Articles By Sharing With Others

When you read a great poker strategy article, share it with your friends via social media or your study group. Get the feedback from others and expand upon the ideas discussed within the article. Content creators try to often include the most relevant and hard hitting strategy bits, and leave off the smaller, maybe not as glamorous, pieces. With your poker pals, you can dive deeper into any skill or area discussed within a great article.

Plus, sharing with others is a way to help your fiends grow in their skills, and helps develop a more solid friendship.

Learning From Forums By Responding With THE ANSWER

Too many people respond to forum posts and questions with unhelpful one sentence answers. These offer little benefit, and due to their brevity cannot prove the author's point. One sentence is more like just their opinion on whatever area discussed.

I can't tell you how many times I've seen a question and answer stream take this form:

- Question: I was in the SB versus a super LAG MP player with statistics at 45/28 over 300 hands. I hadn't 3bet him up to this point but he opened to 4bb's, more than his standard 3bb's. I was dealt A4o. The CO and BTN both folded to me and the BB is very nitty and will fold to most 3bets without KK+. Is this a profitable spot to 3bet bluff?
- Answer: Fo' sho.

What you need to do is think through the question you want to answer and answer it as completely as possible. Don't just give the answer that first comes to mind. Backup your ideas and opinions with proof (in the form of history or mathematical proof or something else concrete).

Treat your answer like it's THE ANSWER – it's the end-all, be-all to the question asked. No further answers are necessary now that you've responded. Of course, you will get responses from others. Respond to these responses. You will find that others will see things you didn't see, and now you get another opportunity to learn more about the given subject.

The next chapter covers much more on "being the teacher."

Learning From Coaching By Coming Prepared

You hired your coach for a reason, correct? You respect his opinion and you know that what he teaches you will be of value to your game and skillset. Then for every coaching session, you must come fully prepared.

In the days leading up to the session, send your coach your most recently played hands so they can go through them and find leaks ahead of time. Send them strategy questions you may have and particular hands you had a difficult time with.

Also, play your poker sessions with the lessons your coach taught at top of mind. Use what your coach is teaching you and report to him how things are shaping up.

Do all the homework assigned by your coach. Read the articles assigned, watch the videos assigned, run through your database as assigned . . . do all the steps your coach asks you to do. Take copious notes on everything, then report your findings.

A coach is most confident in their student's chances of poker greatness when they are actively demonstrating they are taking to heart their coach's teachings. And of course, you will get the most out of the money you paid for coaching by doing everything they ask of you.

Learning From Online Courses By Finishing Them

This one is nice and simple. You bought the course . . . finish it. Get all you can from the materials made available, whether videos, audio recordings, group coaching sessions or pdf handouts. The course creator made everything to work in conjunction, and getting just ½ way through the content might only give you like 25% of the knowledge within.

If necessary, do something like a 30-Day Challenge to help you get through it. You bought the course because you knew it would benefit your game, so a challenge may spur you to completion. (I love utilizing a great reward to spur myself to completing courses, so find a great reward)

Action Step #26 – Learning More From Poker Content

With the next piece of poker content you consume, use at least two steps discussed here to get more from your time with it.

- '7 Steps to Poker Book Learning PDF'
- Questions and Requests
- Note Taking
- Take a Leadership Role
- Sharing with Others
- Respond with THE ANSWER
- Come Prepared
- Finish It

Learning From Poker Strategy Content

* * * *

Speaking of getting active with your studies, in the next chapter I discuss achieving the greatest state of activity in the realm of poker studies: teaching poker to others.

— 24 —
Teaching Poker To Learn

> "While we teach, we learn."
> –Seneca

When we teach a concept, whatever the concept or area of study, there are 4 benefits we gain from it:

1. A Greater Understanding of the Subject Matter

To teach something, we must fully understand it. The test of how well we understand a concept is if we can teach it to somebody so they can use it in their lives.

If you can explain a poker concept like 3betting to your Aunt Susie well enough so she can apply it and blow the table away with well-timed and perfectly sized 3bets the first time she sits at a table, then you probably understand the concept very well. If you can teach your ten-year-old nephew Johnny what an opening range is and how it must widen as his position at the table gets later, and he fully understands and stacks you at the next family home game, then you must understand that concept as well.

When you're responsible for teaching something to others, then you naturally work harder to understand the material. Reasons for this include: not wanting to appear a fool, not wanting to fail in the teaching task or to simply do the best job you can and to give your students the best shot at understanding the material. Whatever the reason, most teachers feel compelled to know the subject matter backwards and forwards. (from a study published in 'Memory and Cognition' in 2014)

The experience of teaching also builds your knowledge over time because of the questions and insights your students give you. Students react to what you're teaching in different ways. Some will get it straight off the bat, and that is great. Others will ask question after question or need a different explanation, one that appeals to them and that they can grasp. These interactions will cause you to think about and explain the material in different ways. This rethinking of ideas and creating different explanations will further help you ingrain the material in your brain.

2. Improved Social and Communication Skills

As a teacher, you work with others all the time, so social and communication skills will naturally improve. And obviously, to communicate ideas, the person you speak to needs to understand what you say and it helps if they can relate to you. If they don't, you're forced to change what you're saying or act differently to find a way for them to understand. Teaching makes you a better communicator.

3. Increased Self-esteem and Self-confidence

When you teach, the element of emotions comes into play. You don't want to be embarrassed by any lack of knowledge and conversely, you feel a sense of satisfaction and a bump in pride when your students understand a concept and can put it to use in their games. Successfully teaching something validates all the hard work you put into studying the topic for yourself. The emotions involved in teaching help you work harder to understand the material.

4. Personal Growth Through Challenging Oneself

This last benefit is very simple; the more you do, the more you can do. When you challenge yourself to do new things, the better you get at doing things you've not done before. This is a skill. Accomplishments come easier to those who have accomplished in the past.

I started this whole Smart Poker Study thing off with writing a blog. Never wrote one before, but I wrote papers in high school and college, so I knew the basics of communicating through the written word. The blog led to making some videos.

Never did those before, but just got started and now I do poker training videos. This led to the podcast. Always loved podcasts, never did one before, but I made my first podcast just over a year ago and I'm still going strong. I haven't written a book before, but now you're holding my first.

All these things were new to me once, and doing one led to the next which led to the next and so on.

If you've never taught and don't know how, that doesn't matter. Just challenge yourself to something new and do it!

How You Can Practice Teaching Poker

Now, I don't want you to label yourself a teacher or a coach until you feel you're ready for that kind of commitment. For now, even though you are not a coach (yet), you can act like one in your interactions with others. Here are some areas you can teach others what you know about poker:

- Lead Study Groups (the 7th of 25 study techniques from chapter 18)
- Post THE ANSWER in Forums (discussed within "Forums" in chapter 23)
- Make Videos
  - This might be a scary thing; putting your hand histories and thoughts out there for others to watch and comment on, but so what. Just do it!
  - Plan the concept you want to teach. You can even script the whole thing out if you want. Record the video and watch it back to make sure there are no mistakes.
  - Put your video out there for the world to see on YouTube, Vimeo or within the SPS Facebook Group. Everyone there is pretty cool and any kind of feedback you get will only help improve your game and the understanding of the concept you teach.
- Create a Blog
  - Like making videos, writing a blog can be daunting for people. But blogs can turn into great things as it did for me.

- Select a short, catchy, easy to remember name. (Sorry, Smart Poker Study, Red Chip Poker, Float the Turn and Cardrunners are all taken.)
- Go the easy route and just use Square Space for your site and domain, especially if you don't have website building experience.
- Post your first article on whatever topic you feel comfortable discussing, then release more on a consistent basis. Consistency is Key (in studying, playing, writing, podcasting, streaming, etc.). The only way you will build a brand and get eyeballs on your stuff is to continue producing.

Beyond these four, there are other avenues of teaching like guest-posting, paid-for articles, podcasts, books, webinars and online courses. You have to start somewhere though, and starting small and building upon little successes will take you who knows how far.

Action Step #27 – Teaching Poker To Learn

Make a poker strategy video on any concept you feel confident in, and post it in the SPS Facebook Group: http://www.smartpokerstudy.com/discuss.

Just do it!

Choose any concept you want, as short or as long as you want it to be. Your goal is to simply teach a concept. Maybe it's about cbetting profitably, or 3betting or defending the blinds. Whatever the topic, just create a video to teach your knowledge to others.

Treat this as a growth opportunity; put yourself out there and learn from doing something new.

* * * *

Don't Forget Your Free Offer
Get the 30-page Workbook for "How To Study Poker"

DOWNLOAD FREE HERE

http://www.smartpokerstudy.com/HTSPfreeoffer

Will You Help Others Improve Their Games With Smarter Studies?

If you enjoyed 'How To Study Poker', would you mind taking a minute to write a review on Amazon? Even a short review helps, and it'd mean a lot to me. The more positive reviews this book has, the more Amazon will help others see it and hopefully read it.

Please go here to give an honest review:
www.smartpokerstudy.com/HTSPreview

Finally, if you'd like to get free bonus materials from this book and receive updates on my future projects, you can sign up for the Smart Poker Study Newsletter at www.SmartPokerStudy.com

You can also follow me and Smart Poker Study and join in the discussion:
Facebook: http://www.smartpokerstudy.com/discuss
Twitter: http://www.twitter.com/smartpokerstudy
YouTube: http://www.youtube.com/smartpokerstudy
Twitch: https://www.twitch.tv/smartpokerstudy

About the Author

Sky Matsuhashi is a poker player, coach, podcaster and video maker. He started this poker journey with home games back in 2003. This turned into hour after hour in the local cardrooms, until eventually he discovered online poker and never looked back.

His Smart Poker Study Podcast and blog is an online resource for players who are eager to improve their games through concentrated and focused study. Sky has brought his years of experience teaching high school mathematics and English in Japan to the poker world.

He continually challenges himself to be a better poker player every day, and helps his students and listeners to do the same.

Sky lives in Fresno, CA with his wife and two sons.

Made in the USA
Lexington, KY
22 November 2017